Much We[illegible]ill

Dedication

I dedicate this book to the small band of loyal trustees and committee members of the Much Wenlock Windmill Trust. My special thanks go to Maureen for her continued encouragement and advice that made this book possible.

Much Wenlock Windmill

Research into the History of the Stone Tower Windmill

A Socio-economic, Political and Technical Review

... The history of the country mill from feudal times to
the present day presents a facet of history of the
countryside as a whole which might well be more fully
explored by social historians than it has been so far.

Windmills in England
A study of their origins, development and future (p. vi)
by
Rex Wailes
London 1948

M J Norrey

Ellingham Press

2010

Every effort has been made to trace or contact all copyright holders. The author and publishers will be pleased to make good any omissions or rectify any mistakes brought to their attention at the earliest opportunity.

Cover photograph courtesy of Sabine Hutchinson
www.virtual-shropshire.co.uk

British Library Cataloguing in Publication Data

A catalogue record for this book is available from the British Library

ISBN 978-0-9563079-1-0

Published by Ellingham Press

www.ellinghampress.co.uk

Typeset by ISB Typesetting, Sheffield

Printed and bound in Great Britain by MPG Biddles Ltd, King's Lynn, Norfolk

Contents

The author is aware that there are varying spellings of names and places and that early documents can contain conflicting information.

List of Illustrations

Introduction

The windmill is in a prominent position overlooking the town. The hillside with its adjoining small copse and adjacent stone quarry has, through the years, been a regular meeting place and playground for many of the local children. It was a magical place for games of knights, castles and dens, and an ideal venue for winter sledging.

Like many of our generation I and my wife left Much Wenlock to pursue our careers elsewhere and returned to live in the town in 1990. We were dismayed at the changed state of the windmill tower and when in 2002 a preservation trust was set up to safeguard the tower and the hillside flora and fauna, we decided to become involved. The Trustees prepared a project proposal to preserve the stone tower, which was in an advanced state of degradation and a danger to the many visitors to the site. The availability of financial grants to assist the preservation project was subject to a feasibility study.

Although a novice in mill design, as an engineer I was interested in preparing a full technical survey of the structure and so became actively involved with the Trust.

The initial survey revealed many intriguing features that required further investigation, which appealed to my research background. It became apparent that an authentic preservation project could only proceed once a firm date for its original construction was established.

To achieve the objectives set out in Chapter 1 it has been necessary to review the social, economic and political influences in and around Much Wenlock prior to and following the dissolution of the monastery.

Distribution of the monastic land mass and properties post-dissolution (1540) was undertaken by the reigning monarch to the benefit of local lords. The approach to awarding tenancies in the period from feudalism through to early capitalism was a significant element in the creation of power and wealth for local lords.

Amongst the more important properties allocated locally were the two watermills that served the monks. It will be shown that these watermills, and those of the adjoining parish through which the water course ran, continued to be prime assets for the local lords.

J Langdon[1] presents an analysis of the effects original long-term tenancies of the period had on the availability of the landlord's wealth in the longer term.

Improved agricultural efficiencies resulted in larger volumes of grain production which, in turn, required a mill of greater output capacity than the existing watermills.

The introduction of a windmill required a suitable site, access to considerable financial funds and a readily available source of building material, mainly stone and wood. Also required would be a range of experienced tradesmen capable of designing, operating and maintaining a stone tower windmill.

A review of the relevant family background and relationships of the succession of local lords post-dissolution has, therefore, been an essential ingredient in identifying the likely landowners of the Windmill Hill site at the time the windmill was built.

It is not the intention that the book should provide an in-depth review of the technological advances in the milling process, from the early hand-mills through to windmills, as a great array of more authoritative material already exists.

This book is the result of my attempt to resolve the historical background to the stone tower and its date of construction and highlight the need for preservation of the remaining stone tower windmills in their natural state, for the benefit of our agricultural and industrial heritage.

Amongst the many significant issues that became apparent at an early stage of the research was the lack of substance and consistency in authentic documentation relating to landownership, location of land areas referred to, estate accounts records and technical detail of the windmill design and construction. Every estate windmill of the period appears to have been unique in its entirety, even within the same county area.

Chapter 1

Project Objectives

Having acquired the lease on the Windmill Hill site from Wenlock Estates, the present owners, in 2001, the Trust Committee assumed responsibility for managing the hillside with its rich variety of flora and fauna. As the general public has open access to the site, via a designated footpath at the top of the hill and a section of the Jack Mytton Way at the base of the hill, it was essential that the fabric of the Grade II-listed windmill stone tower be secured.

Management of the site, which is immediately adjacent to the Shropshire Hills Area of Outstanding Natural Beauty (SHAONB), is supported by the DEFRA Countryside Stewardship Scheme.

Because of the recent increased rate of deterioration of the tower structure, both internally and externally, the Windmill Trust undertook to secure and preserve the remaining shell.

Looking south towards Much Wenlock town from Windmill Hill (2008).

The primary objective was, therefore, to establish the precise age of the windmill and provide the basis for future authentic preservation of the stone tower.

In order to achieve the primary objective a series of secondary ones were pursued, including the establishment of who was instrumental in having the mill built, why it was built and who actually built it.

Successful completion of the primary and secondary objectives would assist an interpretation of the range, type and size of milling machinery originally installed and the likely configuration of the installed equipment.

The two photographs (1953 upper, 2009 lower) highlight the extent of degradation of the top of the tower and the crenellations that were added to the tower post-1867.

1 *Project Objectives*

The initial stage of preservation commenced April 2006 and was completed during September 2006. This included the removal of the remaining crenellated stonework that was added subsequent to the lightning strike that destroyed the mill in 1850.

The high-level masonry has been rebuilt to secure the loose coping-stones that were becoming dislodged, and therefore a safety hazard.

This photograph shows one of the two remaining oak beams that were situated at a height of 7.7 m (24.87 ft). These two beams have been replaced.

The north-facing doorway prior to installation of new lintels and stonework.

Reinstatement of oak lintels and the damaged areas of internal and external stonework above each of the ground floor doorways and each of the four high-level windows was a further requirement.

View showing new lintels and doors at the north-facing doorway and the repointed external masonry.

Internal view of a new window shutter and the reinstated lintel and stonework.

New doors at the north- and south-facing doorways and four new window shutters have been constructed and installed (2009) and the whole of the exterior stonework repointed.

Future stages of activity envisaged would include installing an internal tower cap, below the roof line, prior to reconstructing the remaining damaged areas of internal masonry. Repointing the entire internal stonework could then take place.

Having secured the whole structure and rendered it weatherproof, it would be desirable to reinstate the floor levels in the tower at the original locations. Access to the interior of the tower would then be possible for viewing the proposed interpretation panels, located at each floor level, showing the likely milling process of the period.

Chapter 2

A Historical Perspective

Much Wenlock, in the county of Shropshire, is a small rural town with a long, important and interesting history. Occupation of the area is considered pre-Roman in origin but early importance results from the founding of the Wenlock monastery and the development of the site of St Milburga's Abbey *c*.680.

Having been destroyed by the Danes the Abbey was refounded in 1080 as a Cluniac priory and took ownership of the town.

The following extract from *The Shropshire Gazetteer – A survey of the County (1824)*[2] encapsulates the town's historic importance:

> ...the famous [Wenlock] monastery, which we have just attempted to describe, has attached to it one of the most important instances of genealogical and biographical enquiries that has perhaps ever engaged the attention of readers curious in such matters. The real origin of the royal family of Stuarts [1603–1714] has long perplexed the most ingenious and indefatigable genealogists; it is therefore, with some satisfaction, that we are able to trace this renowned family to the county of Salop; a circumstance that cannot fail to yield some degree of pleasure to the natives of this district, whose high and noble spirit will prompt them to venerate the name, however their more enlightened views may induce them to reject the principles, of that illustrious house.

The extent of the monastic demesne at Domesday is revealed in the following extract from a publication by J C Anderson:[3]

> Earl Roger hath made the church of St Milburg an abbey. The said church holdeth Wenloch, and held it in time of King Edward, Here are xx hides, of these iii hides were free from geld [Danegeld] in time of King Chnut [Canute], and the rest were geldable. In demesne are nine and a half ox-teams; and other xvii [teams] might be here. Here are xv serfs and ii mills, providing for the monks. Here i fishery. The wood will fatten 300 swine; therein are ii hayes. In time of King Edward the manor was worth £15 [per annum]; now £12.

By the thirteenth century the prior's main tenants in the township included the eight freemen and the 39 burgesses, all of whom paid rent.

During the early part of the fourteenth century the Wenlock family became prominent. Richard de Wenlock's son William de Wenlock of Wenlock and Luton (d. 1392) became a priest and ultimately canon of St Paul's Cathedral, Archdeacon of Rochester and Canon of King's Chapel, Westminster.

William Wenlock (Wyvell) (fl.1384–1415) of Luton and Houghton Conquest (Bedfordshire) and Much Wenlock, son of Nicholas Wyvell and Joan, daughter of Richard Wenlock of Wenlock, married Margaret the sister of John Briton and had sons, Thomas (d. 1429) and John, Lord Wenlock (*dsp** Tewkesbury (1471).

John, Lord Wenlock, Privy Counsellor to King Edward IV and Knight of the Garter owned the estate when it comprised 16 messuages and 84 acres.

It is believed that Wyvell gave the 84 acres and properties in Wenlock to father-in-law Richard who ultimately passed it to William the priest who, it is believed, demised (bequeathed) it to Wenlock Priory.

Records reveal that in 1321 the 'Wyndmulehull' (Windmill Hill) site and a windmill existed in Wenlock, this being the earliest known reference.

During the fourteenth and fifteenth centuries the social climate in England was changing from serfdom to free peasant proprietors. Three main classes of agricultural worker emerged. The first category were serfs (or cottagers), who had little or no land of their own. They were contracted to work for the lord, and also protected by the lord. If the lord sold some land the serf went with it to serve the new master.

The smallholder, or middle-class peasant, had to pay rent and often further in-kind contributions to the lord for their property and land. In-kind payment could be either labouring on the lord's land, providing sheaves of wheat for the mill from his smallholding or a selection of 'best' livestock (see Appendix 4, Item v).

The third category were villeins, the wealthier class of peasant, who invariably had between 20 and 40 acres of land spread around the locality for which they also paid rent and in-kind contributions.

Each of the social classes, however, continued to have the facility of common land.

By the end of the fourteenth century William de Wenlock had made a settlement of his estate, including a windmill, on William Wenlock (Wyvell) of Wenlock. It remained in the family until the following century.

**decessit sine prole*: died without issue.

The fifteenth century witnessed the growing prominence of the local Lawley family. Thomas Lawley and Thomas Wenlock (Wyvell) became joint participants in concluding land grants in and around the township. Thomas Lawley, cousin and heir of John, Lord Wenlock, Privy Counsellor to King Edward IV and Knight of the Garter, succeeded to his lands in Wenlock and Calowton (Callaughton) in 17 Edward IV [1478], the first Lawley to be mentioned in documents relating to Wenlock. John Lawley, the grandson of Thomas, married Agnes Wyvell and united the properties of two great local families.

The Lawley family was now second only to the priory in local affairs.

During the fifteenth century Sir John Wenlock was created Baron Wenlock in the peerage of the United Kingdom; this was the first of three creations.

The Borough Charter, granted in 1468 by Edward IV at the request of Sir John Wenlock, Lord Wenlock for services previously rendered, comprised many significant privileges including non-accountability to the Crown and incorporated with a bailiff and burgesses. The Prior's seigniorial rights were, however, to be retained and recognised.

Sir John's request that a Member of Parliament be returned from the borough had now been granted.

Richard Singer, a local man, was nominated by the Superior House of La Charité as prior from 1486 until his death in 1521. Singer was well-disposed towards the recently chartered borough. He was also connected by marriage with William More, four-time bailiff, possibly an earlier relative of William More, the miller at the Greene Mill in 1595.

J Randall[4] (p. 52) states that a bull (papal edict) of Pope Alexander III of 7 October 1494 'freed the Wenlock house from its subjection to foreign ones, a severance sanctioned by the Pope in 1528'.

Randall (pp. 5-54) also presents a historical account of the [Wenlock] town and its institutions, the royal charters, the royal visits to the town and the affiliations of the Priory through to the dissolution.

Randall continues (pp. 137-40) with a full transcript of the Deed of Surrender to the Crown of the monastery of Wenlock dated 1540.

Following the dissolution changes in the approach towards agricultural production continued to take place. Changes in Wenlock land ownership became a regular occurrence with estates operating profitably as a result of producing commodities suited to the land conditions, on land converted from the medieval strip system. The growing of crops, especially corn, and the rearing of sheep that produced high-quality wool were both cost-effective. A change from feudalism to a capitalist-type society was underway.

Major landlords ultimately became aware that feudalism, the system of governing by landed gentry, who invariably had certain defined obligations to the monarch in return for grants of land, was less attractive than the developing capitalist system. This was a system whereby individuals were encouraged to determine their own destiny through selling their labour and/or the production from their labour, thereby providing goods for exchange or sale rather than just for their own use.

Though the landlord's standing in the community was initially determined by the number of his peasants, with the progression of time landownership became more financially beneficial, so the lords sought to drive out the peasants and withdraw their feudal rights. In so doing they were able to convert more land and property into tenancies which, in turn, provided greater income.

The local lords were largely instrumental in establishing the borough in association with the Crown. The Borough of Much Wenlock 1468–1968 Charter document[5] notes that '...that the liberties should extend to and throughout the parish of the Holy Trinity Church. The Burgesses [to be] free of all duties, customs and tolls'. They controlled the quality and price of all victuals within the borough, they chose the bailiff and the recorder as well as the parliamentary member 'out of themselves or others'. The bailiffs and recorder were vested with criminal jurisdiction with unlimited powers to deal with all kinds of offences and retain all fines imposed on convicted persons.

An example of the role and authority of burgesses in Wenlock is referred to in the following article by J Money:[6] 'Review of local politics in the Birmingham area, in the age of the American Revolution.' (Late eighteenth century.)

> The political traditions of Wenlock were such that the resolutions of the burgesses on this occasion – a discussion on Taverns, Coffee Houses and Clubs – probably indicated not so much a desire for change as their wish to maintain the borough's undisturbed tradition of uncontested elections. The 'free, safe and peaceable exercise of their rights' implied specifically the freedom to go on being represented in Parliament by the Forester family, of whom thirteen, not counting relatives, sat for Wenlock between 1529 and 1885. Thus the resolutions passed by the burgesses were probably more significant for the attention which they attracted in places like Birmingham, than for the novelty of their implications in Wenlock itself.

During the early sixteenth century the Lawley family extended their land ownership. Richard Lawley of Spoonhill (brother of Thomas) became tenant of the demesne tenements and land within and outside the town that was previously the property of Wenlock Priory. Richard also bought the watermills and lands in Bourton and Callaughton (including Spoonhill).

The Bertie family, which was ultimately to have a major influence in the continuing development and ownership of land and property in Wenlock throughout the seventeenth century, had returned to England from their twelfth-century exile in France.

The Bertie family comprised seven distinct lines: of Abingdon; Ancaster; Bersted; Kesteven; Lindsey; Uffington and Weston.

Thomas Bertie (d. 1555) ('Mr Bert'), son of Robert of Bersted in Kent, was an acknowledged stonemason in the building trade '[that] flourished primarily because the dissolution of the monasteries released vast amounts of building material for the "new men" to use'.[7]

He also became the master mason for Henry VIII's coastal defences and had responsibilities for maintaining the fabric of Winchester Cathedral. He was also instrumental in the building of Calshot and Hurst Castles.

Stonemasonry continued within the family as the Bertie of Ancaster deposits for 5–26 April 1588 reveal, under Works and Buildings Accounts,[8] 'to digging stone from "the Valdey" (site of Vaudey Abbey) and to work on the new brewhouse and the new windmill at Grimsthorpe'.

The Lawley family involvement in local land and property ownership continued through to the late seventeenth century. Parcels of tenanted land and properties were systematically assembled into estates, thus creating a limited number of the larger landowners. These large landowners often had a direct association with the reigning monarch. The informal enclosure of land by both large and small landowners continued to take place.

Amongst the more important properties acquired by the Lawley family were the two watermills that had served the priory estate (see entries for 1595 – Appendix 3).

Extracts from transcripts of limited available historical records of when and to whom the priory estate assets were to pass are included in Appendix 4.

Following the sale of monastic properties by the Crown during the sixteenth century, land enclosure changed from an informal arrangement to a more forced event led by wealthy landlords. Patronage of the monarchy was no doubt a major factor in the subsequent creation and local involvement of wealthy landowners. It was a succession of these same wealthy landowners that owned the site known as Windmill Hill.

The paper by J D Nichol[9] provides a comprehensive review of the machinations surrounding the local social and political activity during the period 1780 to 1832, a period when major landlords were intent on gaining parliamentary representation of the borough.

Nichol notes that the eighteenth-century political history of Wenlock mirrored its social and economic development. Nichol also provides an account of how burgesses and bailiffs influenced social and political affairs in the borough during the period. Specific reference is made to the large part that ale houses played in local elections. Nicholl highlights the conflict for control over the borough which was 'more concerned with prestige than politics' and identifies the role undertaken by the town clerk in administering the day-to-day control of the borough and the records 'around which any legal disputes revolved'.

Until the introduction of the Municipal Corporations Act (1835) the borough enjoyed an unusual privileged position amongst the boroughs of England. The most obvious impact of the 1835 Municipal Corporations Act on the borough was the loss of its detached parts which amounted to more than a third of its territory. The borough was finally disfranchised in 1885.

Active boroughs created thriving markets and fairs, both bringing much needed income to the area, particularly for the lords, who were able to impose a toll upon those that used them.

Markets were established with the monarch's authorisation, for a fee, and the merchants were allowed various economic and judicial privileges. Fairs, on the other hand, were held at regular intervals and tended to offer a wider range of goods than normal markets. Fairs were normally held only in chartered towns.

The Much Wenlock fair was noted for the trading of locally reared stock. Records of a fair held in the 1630s reveal that buyers and sellers of stock were mainly local tenant farmers.

In 1631 Charles I reconfirmed Henry VIII's Charter of 1547 that was originally granted by Edward IV in 1468 under the name 'Bailiff, Burgesses and Commonality'.

Charles I included the following clause: '...though not to prejudice the Much Wenlock manorial leet (Sir Roger Bertie's Liberties) but expressed no protection for other court leets functioning in the borough'.[10]

The significance of the Lawley/Bertie family involvement on Wenlock's land and property during the seventeenth century is detailed in Appendix 4, Items ii) and v) respectively.

Development of the town throughout the fifteenth to the seventeenth centuries resulted in a significant increase in population, rising to in excess of 1000 by the year 1695. Consequently there was a growing need for increased food production. The rapid increase of population after the mid sixteenth century was accompanied by an expansion in both volume and range of trades pursued locally, including cloth manufacture, stonemasonry, carpentry, wheelwrights, blacksmiths and agriculture workers. Merchants were becoming established and a wider variety of commodities became available. Local dairy produce, especially cheese, was a speciality at most fairs.

Landlords had begun to engage agricultural workers as wage-earners, to produce for profit instead of for revenue, i.e. capital profit instead of feudal rent. Lords were now attempting to regain direct management of their demesnes and watermills, having previously offered them as tenancies, in order to maximise estate income.

By 1534, through an Act of Henry VIII, decayed farms were rebuilt and fixed proportions of land were made available for growing corn and for pasture land primarily for sheep grazing.

Towards the end of the sixteenth century land and property were being transferred, during lives, to chosen heirs.

Historical records of milling, particularly corn milling, in Shropshire are sparse even though the county was a popular area for growing barley. The county was also known for its extensive woodlands and pastureland as well as for rearing sheep that provided high-quality wool. The Lawley family had a vested interest in sheep farming. Wool production had become an important cottage industry and was one of England's major exports to the continent during the late medieval period. As a result of increased export demands for high-quality wool, extensive areas of arable land were used specifically for sheep rearing. Special sheep walks, or runs, were created; consequently landlords sought to acquire even more land for grazing. H D G Foxall[11] identifies a designated sheepwalk in Wenlock township on his Tithes Apportionment Map of 1847, plot 320. Peasants also provided basic wool products that were purchased and then refined by drapers. Expansion of the Flemish wool trade and the resultant rise in the cost of English wool had provided landlords with an additional major source of income.

Thomas Lawley, grandfather of Ursula, was an active member of the Merchant Staplers or Merchants of the Staple, an English trading company established to control the export of English raw wool until exports were banned in 1614. Initially, the company provided an important source of funding for the English Crown. The Merchants' involvement declined as domestic cloth production increased and the export of raw wool diminished, mainly as a result of the introduction of the Cockayne project. William Cockayne's plan was for dyeing and dressing the raw wool prior to export to the Netherlands, thus increasing the sale price. The project failed in 1614 and foreign purchases virtually ceased by 1617.

In the early seventeenth century freeholds and leaseholds superseded copyholds (medieval land tenures) with leases often covering three lives. The Lawleys continued to lease property throughout the eighteenth century for both single lives and ninety-nine years (see Appendix 4, Item v).

Social, cultural and economic changes continued to take place throughout the early Stuart period (1603–1714). The gentry invariably incurred increased expenditure, often to the Crown, in order to maintain their social standing, whilst additional rental income options were restricted because of the previously dispensed grants of long leases.

With the advent of the English Civil Wars (1641–51) the gentry – major landowners – experienced unprecedented social and economic consequences due to often enforced land transactions perpetrated by the reigning monarch to supplement the nation's purse. Manpower and horses were also provided by the lords.

England liberalised land tenureship by the mid seventeenth century. Parliament passed Acts between 1646 and 1660 that abolished the feudal obligations of tenure *in capite* (directly from the Crown).

From the early 1600s stone quarrying became a more significant activity locally as industrialisation gained momentum. Stone and timber were the main building materials of the period though bricks were now being manufactured and became more widely used locally during the eighteenth century.

The emerging capitalist market economy encouraged further development of the local infrastructure. Many large tracts of woodland continued to be sold to raise additional finance for the landowners and mining for coal and iron ore aided the development of iron production processes.

Informal enclosures provided the foundation for capitalist accountability and allowed landlords to use their remaining feudal power – their dominance of the land and of Parliament – to impose greater control over their tenants. Consumerism was now driving the capitalist economy.

R A Bryer[12] states, 'A major debate neglected by accounting historians is the importance of landlords in the English agricultural revolution.' The paper uses accounting evidence from the historical literature to test Marx's theory that, 'from around 1750, England's landlords played a pivotal role by adopting and then spreading the capitalist mentality and social relations by enclosures and changes in the management of their estates and tenants.' Bryer suggests that accounting and other evidence supports Marx's theory that capitalist farmers drove an 'English agricultural revolution' that began in the sixteenth century but took hold from the late seventeenth century. Bryer's paper also states, 'Marx argued that industrial society emerged from long processes of class conflict resulting in the overthrow of the feudal mode of production by the capitalist mode of production.'

Major landowners recognised that by pursuing the extent of enclosure, larger single land areas could be created and, as a consequence, advances in agricultural production methods were achieved. The old inefficient strip system was rationalised with the resultant effect of improvements in productivity along with increased rental values.

The manorial lord's control over his tenants would be further enhanced as ownership of small tenants' watermills was systematically brought under the control of the lord, especially in the period around the 1670s, when corn increasingly became the staple commodity in local markets. Tenant farmers were now under an obligation to use and to pay for their crops to be milled at the lord's mill.

The increased demand for milled grain during the seventeenth century was accompanied by a new major development that was taking place: construction of the more robust and versatile stone tower mill. Stone tower mills could accommodate larger items of machinery and ultimately benefited from having a cap with sails that could be more readily turned into the prevailing winds, hence allowing the mill to be utilised to a greater extent, giving greater output and providing more income to the manor. They were, however, much more costly to build and maintain.

The advent of the 'soke' (control of milling rights, one of the feudal rights of lordships) further established windmills as a major asset to the lord. A secured income from the mill would have been the financial justification for building it.

A paper presented by I L Donnachie and Norma K Stewart,[13] using material provided by J Reid (of Allness), refers to the cost of a tower mill in 1797 as £200-300. A watermill would have cost £80-100 and a horse mill £70.

The succession of Wenlock's major landowners during the period from the fifteenth to the early eighteenth centuries, namely the Lawley/Bertie/Penruddocke/Gage families, had access to a combination of both the finance and the experience essential for building a stone tower mill.

The Lawleys had earlier used stone from the disbanded Wenlock priory for the construction of dwellings around the manor, including their own dwelling at Spoonhill.

Lady C Milnes Gaskell refers to the local population removing stone from the church (abbey) during the eighteenth and nineteenth centuries.[14]

An abundance of local suitable hardwood was also available to the Lawley family and is likely to have been used in the construction of the tower internals, namely gearing, drive-shafts, ancillary machine items such as hoists, hoppers, sieves, as well as the sails' framework. The close interrelationship between these families became a significant feature in the developing social, economic and political environment locally.

The Bertie family, having previously undertaken stonemasonry work for Henry VIII at Winchester Cathedral and at Calshot and Hurst Castles, used material from the disbanded Vaudey Abbey to build Grimsthorpe windmill in Lincolnshire *c.*1588.

As a result of judicious marriages the Bertie family gained considerable wealth through land acquisition as well as gaining an important political standing, particularly in the Lincolnshire area (J V Beckett[15]). A daughter of William Cockayne had earlier married into the Bertie family.

From the sixteenth century the Bertie family (Dukes of Ancaster), at Grimsthorpe Castle in Edenham (Lincs), were one of several powerful landed gentry in that region. Grimsthorpe was also an area of extensive sheep farming as early as 1584. During the period 1635–8, Robert Bertie (1st Earl of Lindsey) and Sir William Killigrew, an English court official under Charles I and II, were both familiar with the benefits derived from using windmills, as they employed windmills in their attempt to drain the Lincolnshire Fens. Bertie was contracted to drain an area lying between Kyme and The Glen, an area of 36,000 acres, on the understanding that he would receive two-thirds of the reclaimed land. On completion he built houses and farmsteads on the enclosed land.

Sir Roger Bertie, second son of the 1st Earl Lindsey, married Ursula Lawley, daughter of Sir Edward Lawley and granddaughter of Thomas Lawley of Wenlock, uniting two wealthy families. Following the death of Sir Roger, Ursula married Sir George Penruddocke and maintained a financial interest in the Wenlock estate.

Ursula and Sir George Penruddocke's daughter Elizabeth Penruddocke married Joseph Gage of Sherborne Castle and had a son Thomas Gage, 1st Viscount Gage (before 1702, died 1754). Thomas Gage, 1st Viscount Gage, a kinsman of the Lawleys (see Appendix 4, item iv)) became lord of the manor following the death of Robert Bertie, Esq. in 1699. Viscount Gage sold the manor in 1714.

Sparse records exist for both the Penruddocke and the Gage families' involvement in the Wenlock estate properties as they were noted more for their long and distinguished military careers. They were generally referred to as absent landlords.

Between the 1730s and 1830s enclosure was being formally authorised by individual Acts of Parliament as well as through the earlier formal and informal agreements of landowners. Although enclosures assisted promotion of modern farming methods, the wholesale enclosure of agricultural land became more prevalent and, as a result, the smallholders began to lose their common rights, often by unilateral action of landowners. Agricultural wage increases did not match the rise in prices as wild fluctuations in the price of corn were taking place. It is reputed that farmers and millers resorted to profiteering. Agricultural workers, therefore, were amongst the worst affected by the introduction of the Enclosure Acts.[16]

In 1777 approximately 80 per cent of the 704 acres of the Much Wenlock land area was arable, the remainder being open field and common waste. Recordings of enclosure by the Clerk of the Peace, however, were not always taking place as the only record of the disappearance of Farley Common (58 acres enclosed 1818) in Much Wenlock is through a private deed. The enclosure award of Farley Common included, at least, a part of Bradley. Joseph Reynolds and Hannah Mary Rathbone (son and daughter of Richard Reynolds) were participants, with Lord Forester taking the larger share. The Pitt family, with several others, took lesser parts of the apportionment.

Extensive commons remained until the early nineteenth century and some were never enclosed.

Population growth during the nineteenth and early twentieth century continued as local trade and industry developed largely as a result of increasing industrialisation.

Coincident with the destruction of the windmill in the mid nineteenth century, corn milling in Much Wenlock appears to have ceased.

Chapter 3

Secondary Source Material

The chapter comprises a selection of previously published material that provides further insight into the historical background to the Wenlock estate. Progression from the estate's two watermills to one watermill and a stone tower windmill is reviewed.

Socio-economic changes, influenced mainly by legislation and agricultural land distribution during the period from the seventeenth century to the mid nineteenth century – the period during which the stone tower windmill was operational – are discussed below, along with a number of important technological advances in the milling process.

It is considered, however, by the author that the majority of technical innovations presented would not have been available for inclusion in the Much Wenlock mill.

R W Eyton[17] states 'the Domesday notice of Wenlock Manor gives us no intimation of a town therein. The district involved seems to have been purely agricultural.'

In 1066 about 370 people were living around the minster (the Abbey church). Eyton estimated the area of the seven Wenlock manors at Domesday (1086) as 74¼ hides (approx. 9000 acres) producing an income of about £50 a year.

The prior's position as lord of the manor, and landlord, received annual Temporal Revenue which included manorial dues, court receipts and rents – rents from the watermills were a major source of this annual income. As the mills were considered to be the most significant local secular buildings the lord's interests were safeguarded in the courts.

The relationship between the prior, as landlord, and his tenants was not always harmonious. D C Cox[18] refers to a royal writ secured by the eight freemen and 39 burgesses, 'who hold their freeholds of the prior of Wenlock, against their lord the prior of Wenlock, for extorting unlawful tolls'.

Eyton notes that the priory had six watermills operating in 1379 but post-1600, the period during which the Wenlock windmill was constructed and operable, only three had survived with the last one working until the early twentieth century. The three mills have been referred to in historical documents by a variety of names – Masons Myll, the Paper Myll and Greene Myll – and at various locations. Greene Mill, ultimately referred to as the Downs Mill, was the last recorded working watermill in Wenlock township.

Appendix 3 contains an overview of the mills, their locations and the recorded millers at specific dates.

W F Mumford refers to the location of 'a disused mill' to the left when viewed from the lady chapel of the monastery with Downs Farm to the right.[19]

A recent publication by V Bellamy[20] provides an insight into the early history of the priory and notes that 'the powerful Norman earl, Roger of Montgomery...preferring first to reorganise the church here as a Benedictine priory affiliated to the French monastery at Cluny.' Bellamy also reveals that 'relations with the French monastery continued to be close and in 1198 the new prior came direct from La Charité.'

Earl Roger's original priory church was rebuilt during the first half of the fourteenth century. The prior was the major landowner in Wenlock as a result of land being distributed by the monarch under the feudal system and controlled local law and order, as well as fuel and food production, from the time of the Norman Conquest until dissolution of the monasteries by Henry VIII.

Bellamy highlights how the monks managed woodland and farms themselves and let land to tenants as well as having an involvement '...in both agriculture and industrial operations such as mills and iron-founding'.

Before the introduction of the potato in Tudor times (1485–1603), bread was the staple food for the majority; flour was no doubt milled locally at the two demesne mills and often by individual freehold tenants and possibly by some feudal serfs using less sophisticated mills than watermills, namely hand mills or the less labour-intensive horse mills.

The watermills serving the monastery up to and beyond the dissolution may have fallen into the category identified by R Holt[21] who described Shropshire as being '...one of three counties where mills described in the Domesday Book were referred to as winter mills because they were considered to be marginal enterprises on inadequate streams'.

Holt reflects that '...during the thirteenth century in particular there were a large number of mills, not under the direct control of the manor. These were independent mills...though not so common after 1300 a large number survived the less favourable conditions of the fourteenth and fifteenth centuries.'

However, these early independent mills, of limited and irregular output capacity, inefficient production and providing limited profitability, would have satisfied the needs of small tenants or a serf-owner.

Holt also reveals that 'through their legal right to force their tenants to use the manorial mill, and to extort an excessive fee for the privilege, the owners [lords] could ensure profitability of the investment that only they could make.'

Mills and milling in and around Much Wenlock, as with most other townships at the time, remained an important part of estate development. Watermills, the forerunners of windmills, were therefore a significant and integral part of socio-economic development of the manor and its local community.

Records reveal that two watermills, for corn milling and a paper mill, were operating on the estate in 1647 on land owned by the Lawley/Bertie family (see Appendix 3).

A parish watermill sited at Wigwig has been referred to as a 'fulling mill' (the cleansing and thickening of cloth) which had ceased operating by 1695.

Limited available records allow only for brief reference to the number, precise location and operational dates of the mills in Wenlock manor – see History of Milling in Much Wenlock (Appendix 3) – as the names of the mills appear to have changed over time!

The ever-increasing demand for a staple diet using milled grain was instrumental in mill development.

The change from watermills to windmills necessitated construction of a vertical tower structure; initially these were wooden post mills, then smock mills, which were ultimately superseded by the more robust stone or brick tower mills. The Grimsthorpe mill (in Lincolnshire), built in the late sixteenth century, was an early example of a stone tower mill.

Amongst the major differences in construction and operation from watermills to the windmill was the installation of a vertical *brake-wheel* in the windmill instead of a horizontal one in the watermill.

The *brake-wheel*, the large cogged wheel attached to the *wind-shaft* that carries the windmill sails, is housed inside the tower *cap* – see Schematic Arrangements on pages 54 and 56. The relocation of the *brake-wheel* position resulted in a complete reconfiguration of the remaining internal milling machinery and allowed for an increase in size and complexity of the milling equipment.

Stone towers capable of holding larger, more technologically advanced milling components presumably would also have been more effective in terms of regular production capacity and possibly the quality of meal produced, than the earlier types of demesne watermills and the independent mills.

M Watts in his review of the financial viability of tower mills[22] states, 'that they were relatively complex as well as an expensive alternative to post mills...tower mills were not generally considered a viable economic alternative to post mills until the eighteenth century. There are some interesting exceptions, however...'

The economic welfare of the local community would now be more heavily dependent on the landlord of the period, who would have recognised the need and financial benefits to be gained from having a more robust stone tower windmill.

As new and greater skills would have been required for designing, constructing, operating and maintaining the tower mills, only wealthy landlords could have financed these developments.

Holt (pp. 176-7) presents details of windmill construction costs in the thirteenth and fourteenth centuries. Milton Hall mill in Essex cost £15 4s. 11d. in 1299, and Brandon Mill in Suffolk, rebuilt seventy-five years later, cost £20 8s. 2d.

Ian L Donnachie and Norma K Stewart present a typical construction of 'a large windmill' in the late eighteenth century as £200-300. They also note the cost reflects 'the wright's efforts to construct a mill which was both simple and of high technical standard. The tendency for mills to become larger and more complex was also related to the miller's desire for more space and output.'

Whilst the above costs were indicative of the various periods – 1299 to 1797 – no specific references are made to the output capacity of each mill or to the revenue potential of each unit.

Donnachie and Stewart, however, draw attention to the fact 'that in terms of finance the windmill was never a sound proposition where water was available in plenty'. Whether this conclusion is based on construction, operation and maintenance cost is not clear.

R Holt (p. 123) makes reference to the operational and maintenance problems experienced in tower mills in his statement:

> The regular services of smiths, for instance, were called upon, as it was generally considered essential for certain parts of the mill to be made of iron. Principally these were the *spindle,* usually called the *fusillum,* and the *rynd* or *ynkum* which was the iron fitting that held the upper *millstone* or *runner,* so that it rested on and moved with the *spindle.*
>
> Not surprisingly, the spindle needed to be strong to support the constant weight of the *millstone* running perhaps at over one hundred revolutions per minute.

A E P Shillingford refers to the type of millstone used.[23]

> The Derbyshire Peak stone is a form of hard sandstone used for grinding coarser grain such as oats and barley and French Burr, made up of small pieces of stone, shaped, matched and set in cement and backed with plaster of Paris and bound with iron hoops.

Each stone would be about 4 ft in diameter, 12 in. thick when new and weighing approximately one ton.

Windmill caps that were capable of turning the sails to benefit from changing wind directions were a major development in mill design and construction.

R Wailes refers to caps as '[being] the distinguishing feature of tower mills, each having its own traditional designs, though now that so many mills have disappeared it is not easy to tell what was the tradition for a given area.'[24]

R J De Little[25] believes that the caps of Shropshire mills were similar in design to the typical Cheshire cap. A photograph of the restored Gayton Mill cap (Cheshire) is presented in Chapter 5, p. 52.

A E P Shillingford[26] provides a detailed description of a timber cap construction. No record of the cap design of the Wenlock mill is known.

Up until the end of 1695 the Windmill Hill, and presumably the windmill itself, remained under the ownership of the Bertie family as the Last Will and Testament of Richard Coundley (senior), dated 1685, refers to his holdings, which includes the mills, 'I now hold of my landlord Esquire Bertie.'

The Demesne Land Survey for the manor of Wenlock, dated 1717,[27] included as Appendix 4, Item v), presents details of landowners, tenants and also the acreage, type of land (arable, meadow or pasture) and yearly rental charges incurred. An entry on page two of the survey document contains a reference (carrying the date 1714) to the existence of the windmill and two water grist mills occupied by Richard Counley [Coundley] (Junior). A further entry in the document refers to 'the Standhills wherein is the windmill etc' with tenants Mr Richard Parsons, Isabel Smart, widow, and John Roberts.

The Rocque's Map of 1752[28] depicts a windmill in the vicinity of the Windmillhill Field. The precise location of the mill shown on Rocque's map cannot, however, be established. As there are no visible remains of any previous structures sited on the hill it must be concluded that his map refers to the stone tower mill.

H D G Foxall[29] in 1847 defined the Standhills as being an area 'of fields where stone was quarried' and places the Windmill Hill site (plot 259) adjacent to the Standhills Meadow plot (203). The location of the stone tower windmill on Windmill Hill is recorded as plot 260 within plot 259, covering an area 5½ yards square (or 30¼ square yards or 1 perch).

A Contemporary Survey of Windmills in Shropshire[30] records Much Wenlock tower mill as 'the earliest known date (pre 1750) of all Shropshire Mills of which the tower remains – last date of operation (*c.*1890)'. The windmill in fact had ceased operation in 1850, the date the tower was reportedly struck by lightning.

Sir Watkin Williams Wynn, Bart. had been the owner of the Windmill Hill site since 1719 with Benjamin Ainsworth as occupier of the land.

Between the 1730s and the late 1800s, the social and economic climate of rural England continued to change. The wild fluctuations in corn prices during the 1790s apparently stimulated profiteering by farmers and millers, with the poorer members of the community bearing the brunt of it as wheat prices trebled.

Parliamentary legislation, namely the Enclosure Act and the Board of Agriculture Act (1889) (Tithe Apportionment), along with the progress towards industrialisation ultimately had an effect on further developments and utilisation of local estate mills.

A typical example relating to enclosures in Shropshire[31] is the valuation of Sir Watkin Williams Wynn's Much Wenlock estate *c.*1770 by John Probert which included a recommendation that 'a reorganisation of the farms that included enlargement of the biggest ones'. Probert also advised 'a cautious canvas of other freeholders about the desirability of enclosing Westwood Common by Act, under which the inconveniently interspersed freeholders of Williams Wynn and others could be consolidated; that part of the programme, however, was achieved until 1814.'

Whether the windmill tower itself was owned by Sir Watkin Williams Wynn and included in John Probert's *c.*1770 valuation of the estate remains unclear.

Being a period of relative prosperity for British agriculture and continued population growth, stimulated locally by industrialisation, the increase in demand for food had the effect of raising prices, rents and land values to unprecedented levels and further encouraged enclosure.

The process of enclosure of open land (with hedges, ditches, fences, etc.) that had formerly been subject to common rights created larger estates. Coincident with increased enclosure, ownership of the major local estate appears to have stabilised. Small-scale tenant farmers found it more difficult to implement evolving farming innovations on their scattered strips of land.

When the 'common' land became enclosed, 'it destroyed the economic independence of cottagers who now had to depend on their wages alone, being forced to sell their livestock – the very means which had kept them from sinking into absolute poverty.'[32]

Chapter 4

Structural Survey Data

The recorded data include measurements of all significant features within and around the tower, namely the physical relationship of doorways, windows, floor levels and beam pockets. Close examination of the coping-stones was undertaken.

The recorded detail is continually being assessed to ascertain how known basic components of a milling process of the period would have been arranged within the tower. Diagrammatic forms of the relevant recorded detail are presented below along with schematic representations of likely major milling component configurations.

The stone structure has an external diameter at the base of 6.16 m (20.15 ft) and a nominal 3.8 m (12.5 ft) internal diameter, giving a wall thickness of 1.2 m (4 ft).

The tower is battered to a height of approximately 7.0 m (23 ft) where the wall thickness is 0.45 m (1.48 ft). The wall, externally and internally, then extends parallel to a height of 9.0 m (29.5 ft).

The top of the tower stonework, at the coping-stones, has external and internal diameters 4.7 m (15.45 ft) and 3.8 m (12.5 ft) respectively giving a wall thickness of 0.45 m (1.48 ft).

The external and internal wall construction throughout the tower comprises irregular-shaped and irregular-sized limestone blocks with limestone rubble infilling.

The mill appears to have had four floor levels inclusive of the cap floor.

Indications are that both ground floor doorways had two opening doors of typical seventeenth century construction, which were 'usually made from simple boards (planks), with external doors cross-boarded for strength'.[33]

The doorway outer dimensions are 1.22 m (4 ft) wide, 2.13 m (7 ft) high with the doors recessed in from the outer wall by 0.46 m (1.58 ft) at the base and 0.38 m (1.25 ft) at the top. The internal dimension of each doorway is 1.35 m (4.4 ft).

The tower has four window apertures; two are located within the first floor area having orientations of east-north-east and due west. The external openings are 3.6 m (11.8 ft) above ground level with external dimensions of 0.6 m (2 ft) and 0.4 m (1.3 ft) wide. The two high-level windows in the third floor area have orientations of north-east and south-west at 7 m (23 ft) above ground level. The external openings are 0.8 m (2.6 ft) and 0.6 m (2 ft) wide.

There are two identical doorways at ground floor level, more or less diametrically opposite, in a general southerly and northerly orientation. The function of each beam pocket in the ground floor area has yet to be established. However, the first floor boarding could have been carried from lintels situated in the beam pockets directly on top of the internal lintels at each doorway. The stairway to first floor may have been supported partly by timbers protruding from the smaller pockets around the inner wall surface.

One of the two remaining high-level beams is shown. The lime mortar skim in the second floor area has a nominal thickness of 10mm. Below it is a partially bricked-up aperture in which one of the two low-level beams had been situated. To the right-hand side of the low-level window opening can be seen an area of stonework that is part of the south-easterly orientated chimney or ventilation shaft with the wood lintel missing. The internal stonework at the two low-level window openings is angled as shown. These would have provided easy access for viewing the surrounding area.

Either side of the high-level window aperture are the elongated pockets referred to on p. 38. Beneath the elongations is the only section of 'surface plaster finish' to the internal stonework.

The first floor boarding would have been carried on a combination of minor beams and existing stonework at 2.3 m. Minor beam pockets are located above the internal doorway lintels.

The first floor level, possibly the *stone floor* housing the *mill stones* are located, appears to have been at 2.44 m (8.0 ft) above ground level.

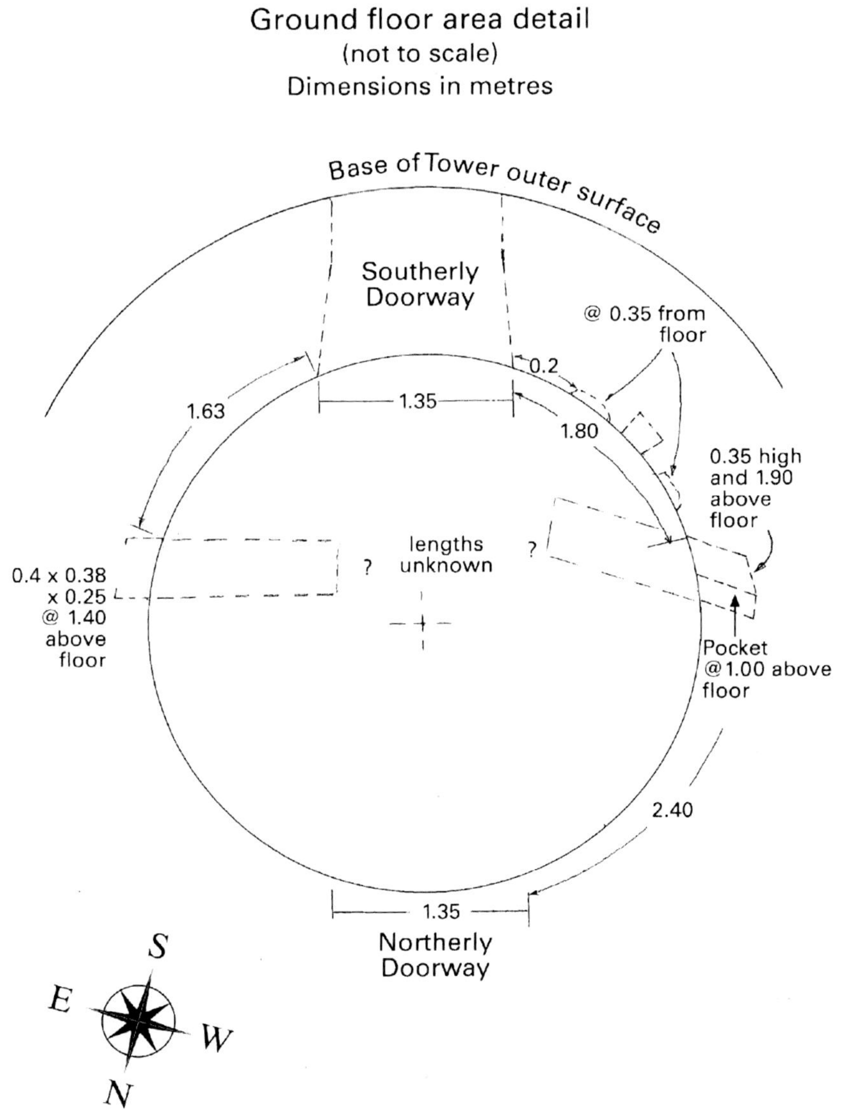

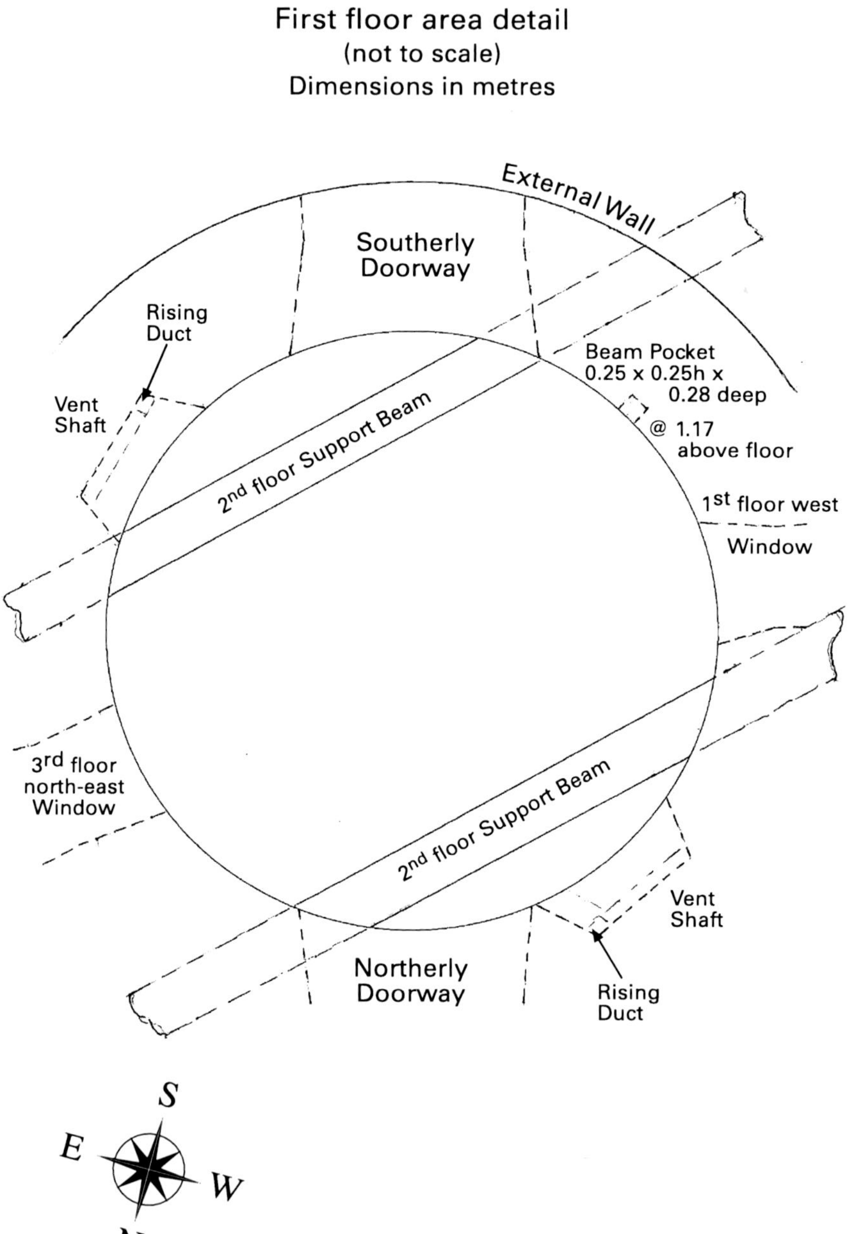
First floor area detail
(not to scale)
Dimensions in metres
External Wall
Southerly Doorway
Rising Duct
Vent Shaft
Beam Pocket 0.25 x 0.25h x 0.28 deep @ 1.17 above floor
2nd floor Support Beam
1st floor west Window
3rd floor north-east Window
2nd floor Support Beam
Vent Shaft
Rising Duct
Northerly Doorway
S
E
W
N

The interior wall has a diameter of approximately 3.9 m (12.8 ft) with an external diameter of 5.7 m (18.7 ft) giving a wall thickness of 0.9 m (2.95 ft).

The internal dimensions of the tower could have accommodated two pairs of *stones* 1.2 m (3.95 ft) in diameter being driven off the *great spur wheel*. The *great spur wheel* is the cogged wheel located at the base of the main *upright shaft* for driving the *stone-nuts*. The *upright shaft* has the *wallower* – the gear wheel at the top of the *upright shaft* – meshing with the *brake wheel*, with the *great spur wheel* at the bottom of the shaft.

Professional opinion, however, differs as to whether the *stones* were *underdriven* or *overdriven* in the Wenlock mill.

Two apertures, being either fire places or ventilation shafts, are located approximately in a south-easterly and north-north-westerly orientation.

The overall dimensions of each aperture at the first floor are marginally different whilst the rising shafts appear to be identical in size (see page 28). The south-easterly orientated opening has three courses of red brick mounted directly on top of the internal stonework that, possibly, carried the first floor timbers. The red brickwork covers the base of the opening which recesses into the tower wall at 0.36 m (1.17 ft). The height from the top of the brickwork to the

This photograph shows the south-easterly orientated aperture without its original wooden lintel.

This photograph shows the north-westerly aperture with, presumably, its original beam in position. Each aperture has a shaft rising up between the tower inner and outer wall stonework and exiting at high level 5.5 m (18 ft) (see photographs on p. 31).

underside of the beam pocket designed to contain the oak lintel (the lintel is missing) is 0.64 m (2.1 ft).

The width at the front of the opening is 0.81 m (2.7 ft) and at the rear 0.38 m (1.25 ft). The diametrically opposite north-north-westerly aperture has a depth front to back of 0.38 m (1.25 ft) with a height from top of the red brickwork to the underside of the existing wooden lintel of 0.71 m (2.33 ft) at the right-hand side and 0.84 m (2.75 ft) on the left-hand side.

The difference between the two apertures results from the north-north-westerly orientated aperture having an additional four courses of brickwork at the bottom right-hand side (facing from the middle of the tower) of the opening of width 0.35m (1.2 ft) and extending from front to back of the aperture.

The front opening is 0.89 m (2.92 ft) wide and at the rear 0.74 m (2.4 ft).

The existing wooden lintel, at the north-north-westerly orientation, is chamfered on the bottom inner surface and has dimensions of 0.13 m (6 in.) × 0.13 m (6 in.).

The cross-sectional area of the rising ducts tapers as they approach the 5.5 m (18 ft) high-level exit to the atmosphere. These chimney or ventilation shaft exits are such that the predominantly prevailing south-south-westerly winds would create an up-draught at the openings, hence assisting ventilation of the *stone floor*.

Internal section of the south-easterly orientated rising duct viewed from below. No apparent visible signs remain of earlier fire/smoke residue; however, there is a possibility that such signs could have disappeared over time.

This photograph shows one of the chimney or ventilation shaft outlets and one of the red brick infill areas on the outer wall.

This feature, located in the first floor area, is an opening through the inner and outer wall of the tower and situated immediately above the south-westerly-facing doorway. The opening, also included on the diagram on p. 34, shows an external quoin of orange/red brickwork with dimensions of 0.36 m (14 in.) × 0.81 m (31 in.) high. This photograph also shows the red brick infill area on the outer wall at the westerly orientation above and to the left of the quarried area

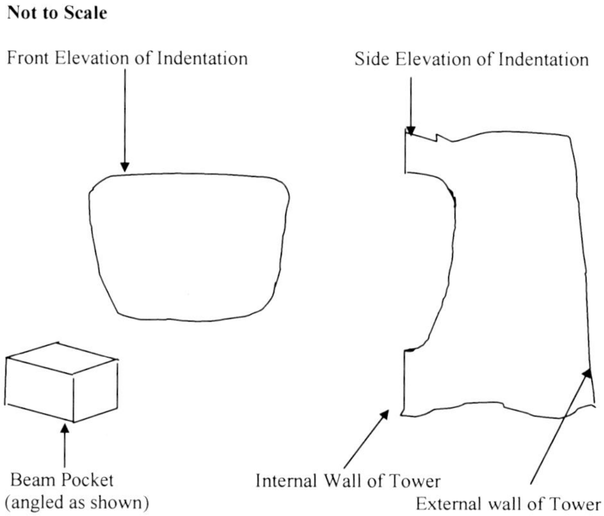

The diagram above depicts an internal structural feature that is not included on the floor area plan for clarity purposes. This structural feature is located at the inner wall surface 1.05 m (3.5 ft) above first floor level, 3.35 m (10.99 ft) above ground level, and 0.5 m (1.65 ft) to the left (viewed from within the tower) of the south-south-easterly-facing chimney/ventilation shaft aperture. This clearly defined indentation in the stonework has dimensions of 0.8 m (2.7 ft) width at the top and 0.65 m (2.1 ft) at the bottom. The indentation from top to bottom is 0.65 m (2.1 ft). The depth of the indentation ranges from 0.1 m (4 in.) (top) to 0.05 m (2 in.) at the bottom. The beam pocket beneath the indentation is 0.076 m (3 in.) × 0.063 m (2.5 in.) and is recessed into the wall, at an angle, to a depth of 0.1 m (4 in.).

The four apertures, currently bricked-up externally with red bricks – see a typical location in the lower photograph on p. 31 – carried two parallel horizontal beams of approximately 0.35 m (14 in.) × 0.35 m (14 in.) section, with a minimum length of 5.2 m (17.1 ft) which extended across the tower and, presumably, protruded through the tower outer wall at a height of 4.6m (15 ft) above ground floor and having an internal diameter of approximately 3.9 m (12.8 ft). The external diameter at this height is 5.2 m (17.1 ft) with walls 0.65 m (2.1 ft) thick.

The beams lay in a north-west to north-east and south-west to south-east orientation 2.3 m (7.6 ft) apart.

The physical dimensions of the beams would have been capable of carrying, at least, the weight of the *grain storage bins* at the *bin floor* situated at the second floor and possibly a *great spur wheel* below which would give an *overdriven* mechanism located within the first floor area.

Immediately above, and slightly offset from the inner right-hand side of the south-facing doorway – when viewed from the centre of the tower internally – at a height of 0.78 m (2.6 ft) above the two major cross-beams or 5.38 m above floor level, is an aperture that contained a lintel (now missing) having dimensions 0.45 m (18 in.) × 0.23 m (9 in.) × 0.11 m (4 in.).

On top of this lintel is a pocket of 0.2 m × 0.2 m (8 in. × 8 in.) protruding through the inner wall to a depth of 0.36 m (14 in.).

At the rear and to the right-hand side of this second pocket is a further pocket of 0.2 m × 0.2 m (8 in. × 8 in.) section extending to the right for a distance of 0.15 m (6 in.).

A further pocket of 0.3 m × 0.2 m (12 in. × 8 in.) then projects directly upwards within the tower wall to a distance of 0.6 m (2 ft).

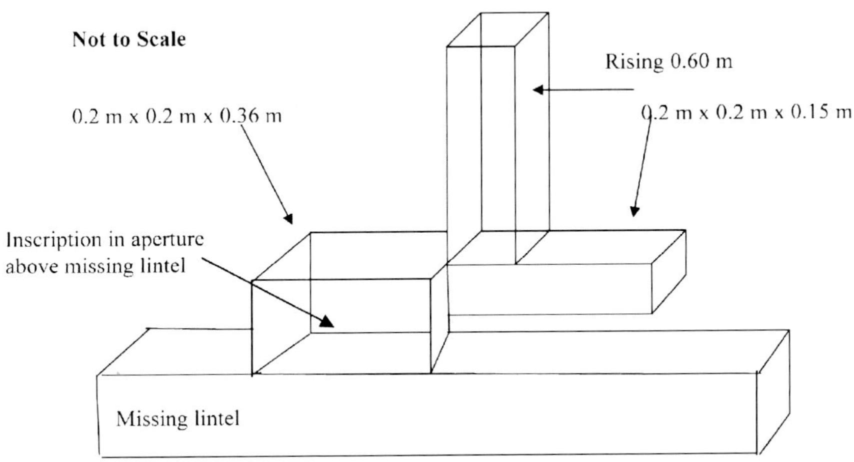

The construction detail of this series of interconnected pockets, at the second floor area.

Second floor area detail
(not to scale)
Dimensions in metres

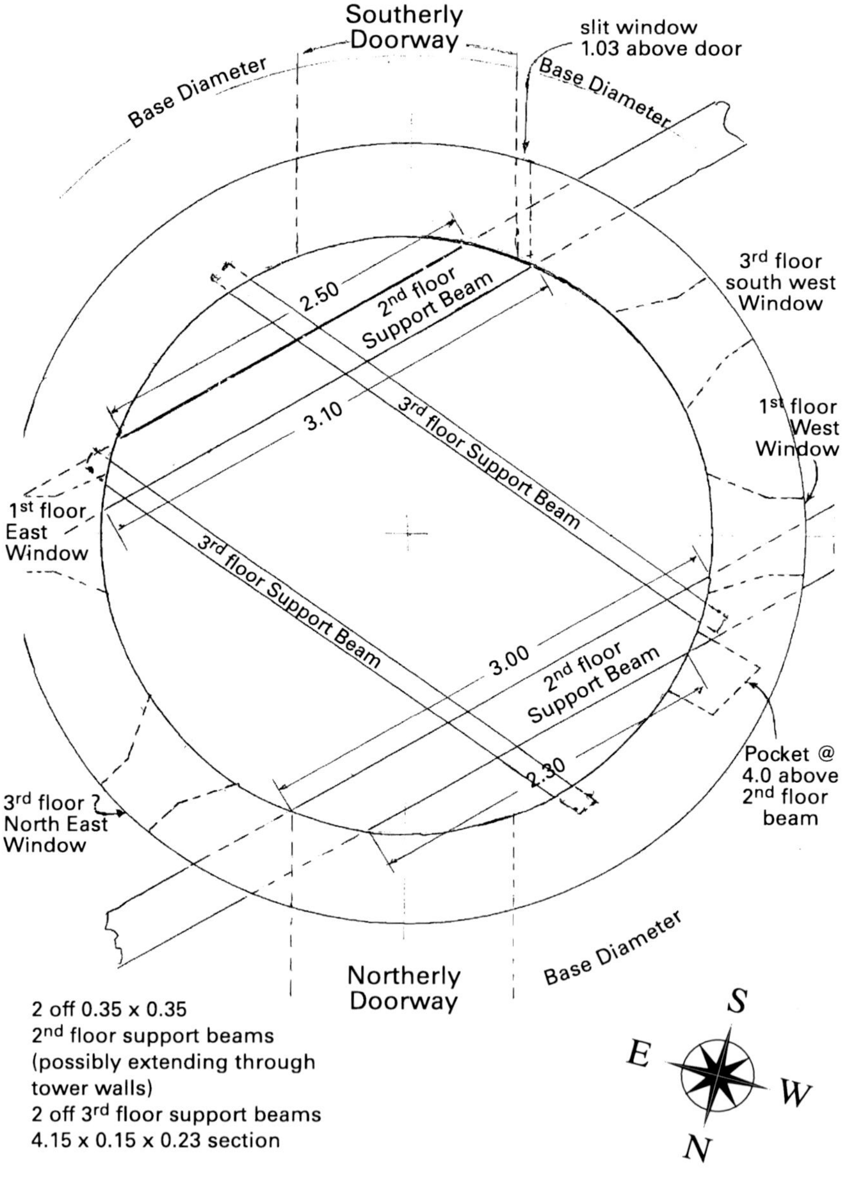

2 off 0.35 x 0.35
2nd floor support beams
(possibly extending through
tower walls)
2 off 3rd floor support beams
4.15 x 0.15 x 0.23 section

Possible application of Pockets @ 3rd floor level
fig 1

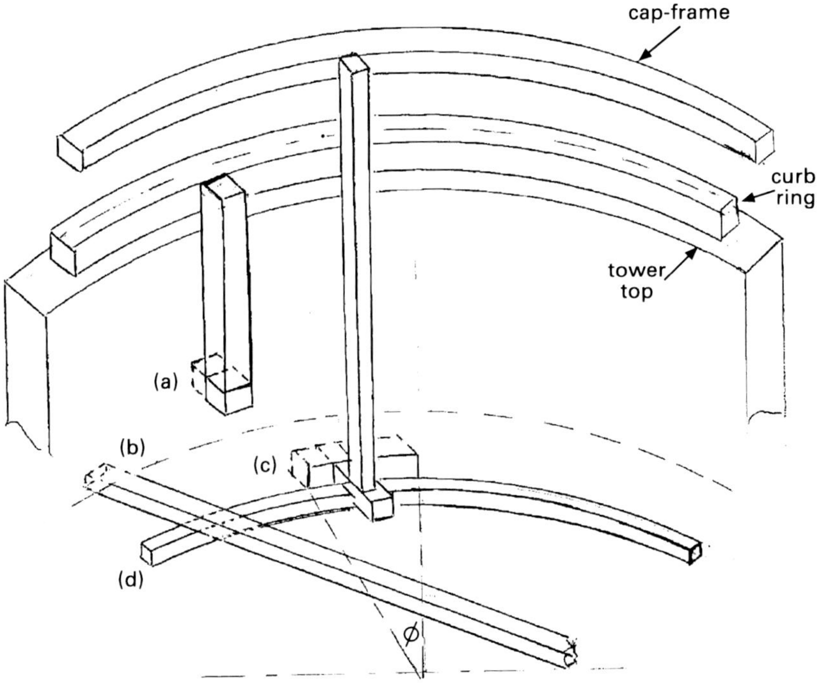

ϕ = 0.4538 rads (26°)

a) one of nine pockets - securing the curb ring

b) floor level supported by the two horizontal beams

c) one of the five recesses – securing the cap frame and allowing for any movement at outer radius of tower

d) ring connecting the five cap frame supports, (5 off)

Around the base of the cap is the cap-frame, running upon the cap-ring of the mill; and the two, if of wood, may run face to face, well greased, and usually with iron plates bedded in the underside of the cap frame: when the cap-ring slides upon the curb the mill is said to have a 'dead curb'.

S.Freese (p29)

Possible cap construction arrangement
fig 2

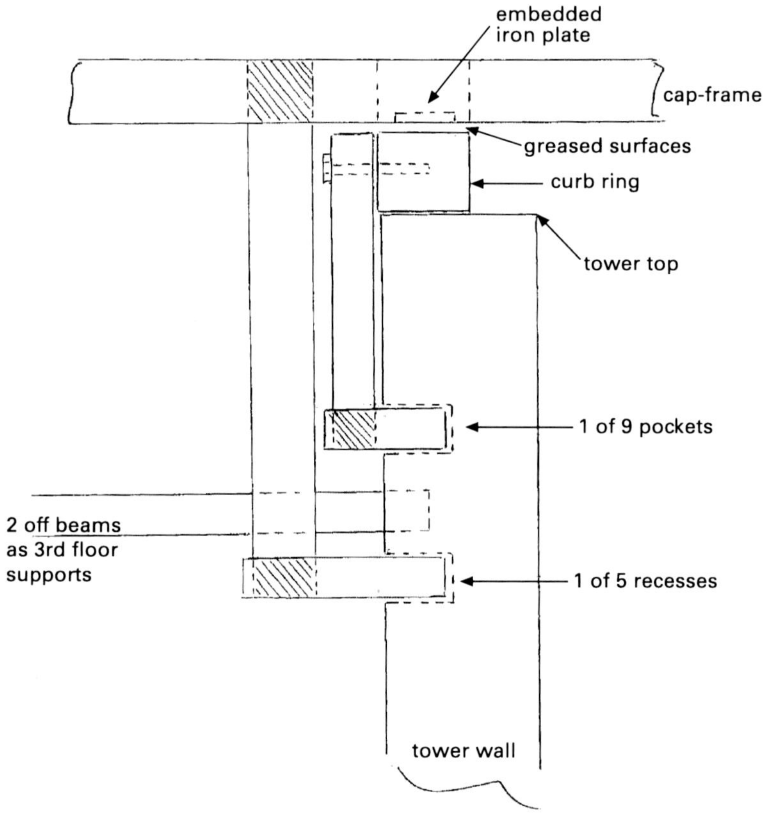

1 of 9 pockets is at 1.12 m from top of tower having dimensions of 0.15 m × 0.18 m

1 of 2 off beams is at 1.3 m from top of tower having dimensions of 0.15 m × 0.23 m

1 of 5 off recesses is at 1.83 m from top of tower having dimensions of 0.46 m × 0.18 m

Possible configuration for securing the curb ring

(not to scale)

Dimensions in metres

fig 3 (fig 1 and fig 2)

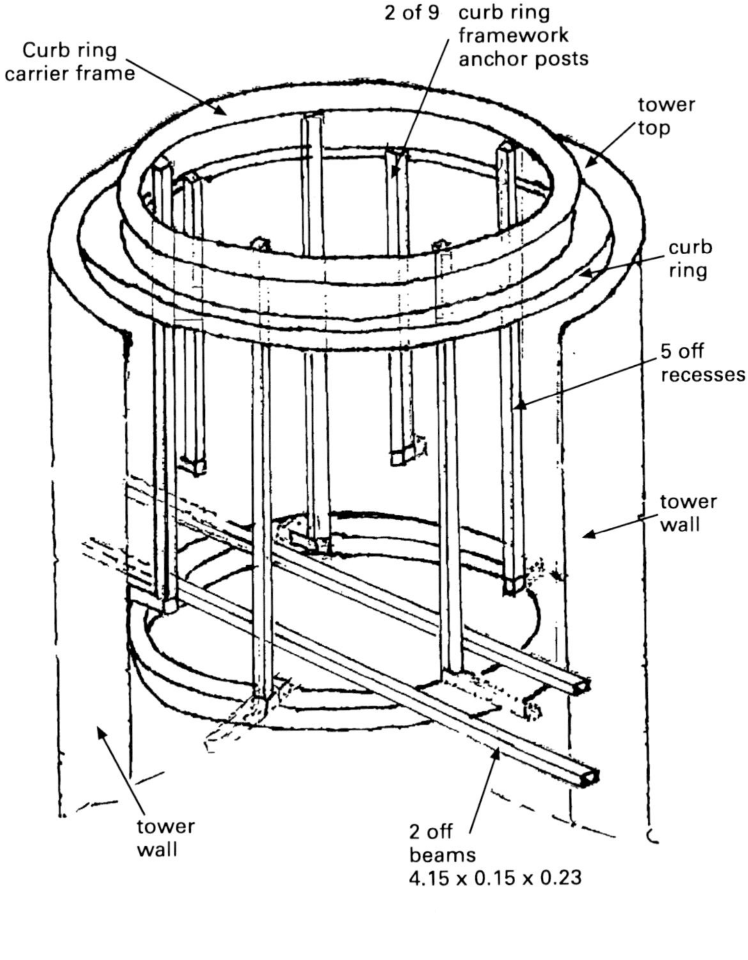

9 off cap frame supports 1.12 from top of tower wall
2 off cross beams 1.3 from top of tower wall
5 off recesses 1.8 from top of tower wall

Placement of Pockets at 3rd floor area

(not to scale)

Dimensions in metres

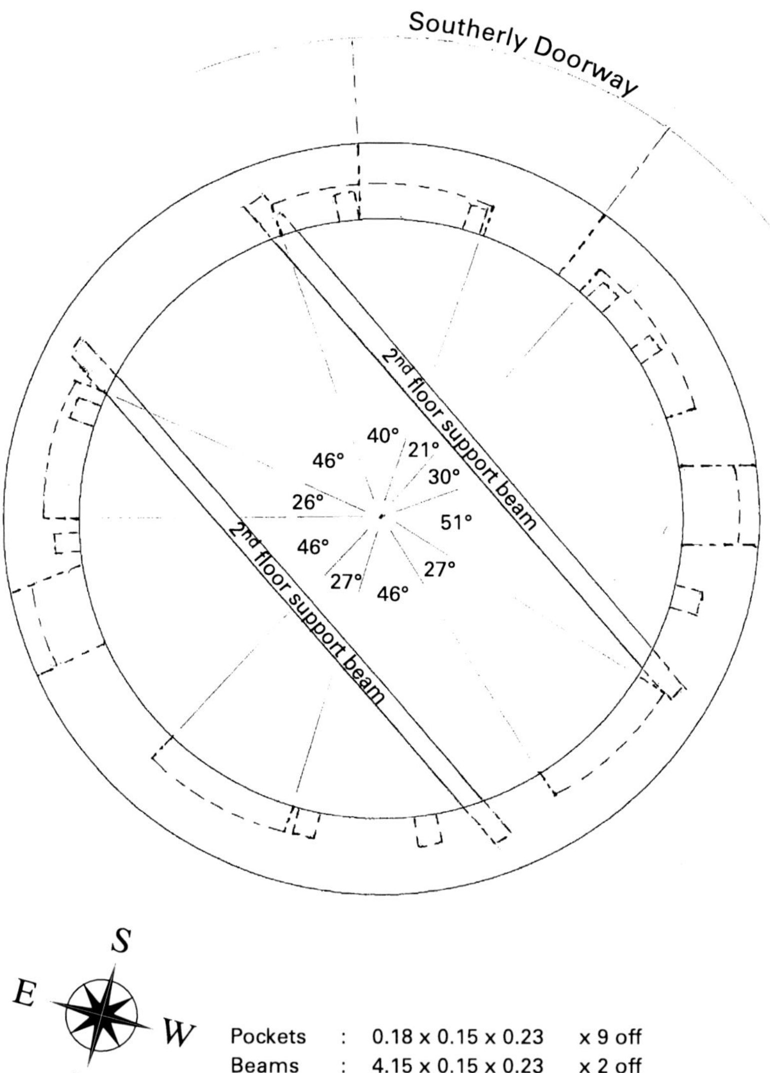

Pockets	:	0.18 x 0.15 x 0.23	x 9 off
Beams	:	4.15 x 0.15 x 0.23	x 2 off
Recesses	:	0.46 x 0.18 x 0.3	x 5 off

The whole of the internal wall in the second floor area, to a height of 1.98 m (6.54 ft), has a rendering of lime mortar 'skim' of nominal thickness 10 mm.

The third floor boarding would have been carried on the two cross-beams shown above.

At the third floor area, considered to have been the *dust floor,* at a height 7.88 m (25.45 ft) above ground level or 1.12 m (3.7 ft) below the top of the coping-stones, there are nine beam pockets of dimension 0.18 × 0.15 × 0.3 m deep (0.58 × 0.5 × 1 ft) located around the inner circumference of the wall.

Located at 7.7 m (24.87 ft) above ground level or 1.3 m (4.2 ft) below the top of the coping-stones there are two oak beams each of 4.15 m × 0.15 × 0.23 section and having a generally north-west to south-east orientation. These two parallel beams, possibly originals, were replaced (April 2007) for safety reasons, prior to commencement of the preservation work.

These two cross-beams in the *dust floor* area were firmly embedded into the tower wall, presumably at the time of original construction and therefore a major feature of the tower *cap* assembly.

There are no signs of a similar arrangement at a lower level, below the 7 m point, within the tower.

A further five regular-sized recesses are built into the inner circumference of the tower at approximately 1.83 m (6 ft) below the coping-stones or 7.17 m (23.16 ft) above ground level, each having dimensions of 0.46 m (1.58 ft) long, 0.18 m (0.58 ft) high and a depth of 0.23 m (0.75 ft).

A typical arrangement of the beam pockets and recesses around the inner circumference of the tower is presented in the photograph on p. 48 and the diagram on p. 38.

Figure 1 and figure 2 on pages 35 and 36 present an interpretation of how a *curb ring* may have been installed in the tower using the nine and the five beam pockets in conjunction with the two cross-beams in situ.

Figure 3 on page 37, a combination of Figs 1 and 2, is not too dissimilar to the arrangement for supporting the *curb ring* – the ring on top of the tower body upon which the *cap frame* rotates – to that depicted by the late Wilfred Forman (1979).[34]

The uniform spatial arrangement of the pockets within the third floor area is superimposed onto the diagram on p. 34, the second floor area detail.

The '9 off' beam pockets (two shown for clarity), noted in Figure 3 above, would have secured the curb ring through vertical uprights to carry an eight-segment wooden curb, to which A Marriott referred.[35]

The position of the *cap* that would have housed the *wind-shaft* and *brake wheel* is included on the Schematic Arrangements.

Two window apertures having a south-west and north-east orientation are situated above the second floor area and would appear to be within the third floor or *dust floor* area, though debate continues regarding the level at which the third floor was situated.

Speculation as to the type, size and physical location of the remaining smaller, yet important, items of milling equipment installed would, currently, be inappropriate.

A pre-dendrology test inspection of the remaining two timbers proved inconclusive – it was suggested, by a dendrologist, that the timber was felled when approximately 12 years of age!

A detailed analysis of the technical survey results and an interpretation of the primary and secondary source material are presented in Chapter 5 Research Summary.

Chapter 5

Research Summary

This summary presents an analysis of the material included in each of the previous chapters and in appendices 1-4 inclusive.

Successful completion of the primary objective as set out in Chapter 1, namely establishing the precise age of the windmill, provides the basis for future authentic preservation of the Grade II-listed stone tower.

In order to achieve the primary objective a selection of secondary objectives were pursued. These included establishing who was responsible for having the mill built, why it was built and who actually built it.

Successful completion of the primary and secondary objectives would assist an interpretation of the range, type and size of milling machinery originally installed and the likely configuration of the installed equipment.

To satisfy the objectives it has been necessary to review the local social, economic and political environment, following the dissolution of the monastery, to establish which of the succession of local lords of the manor owned the site when the mill was built. Identification of the landlords over the period post-dissolution of the monastery through to the late seventeenth century has, therefore, formed an important aspect of the research.

Whilst a number of attempts have been made previously, by others, to establish the original date of construction no conclusive evidence has been presented, though the late seventeenth or early eighteenth century was speculated.

An interpretation of the recently obtained technical survey data for the remaining structure is presented below. The author's interpretation, in conjunction with technical material previously published by others on the development of stone tower windmills in Britain, partially satisfies the secondary objectives.

A brief reference to the existence of St Milburga's Abbey around which the historic town of Much Wenlock developed is included in Chapter 2 A Historical Perspective.

The effect of monastic control on the use of the land mass surrounding Wenlock township, of the township itself and on the livelihood of the indigenous population pre-dissolution of the monastery is briefly referred to. The progression from feudalism to a more capitalist-type society identified the need for, and the result of, changes subsequent to monastic control. Charting the progression has been a significant feature of research into the origins of the windmill.

Recognising the socio-economic, political and financial benefits from having the estate's watermills has also been an essential ingredient of the study. R W Eyton[36] notes (page 261) that in the thirteenth century 'the Prior had Four mills yielding annually £3 17 4', and by 1379 the site of the priory is recorded as having 'six Water-Mills producing an income of £3 0 0' (page 263).

Greater attention, however, is given to the period post-dissolution of Wenlock monastery with particular emphasis on land distribution (ownership) and the opportunities available for wealth creation by local lords. The effect locally following the introduction of the Enclosure Acts governing the reallocation of the land mass of both the late monastery and Wenlock township has also been considered.

Subsequent to the 'Deed of Surrender to the Crown of the Monastery of Wenlock by the Prior and Convent of Wenlock', in 1540 systematic reallocation of land and existing properties was fundamental to the rise and welfare of future major landlords. Successful land acquisitions provided the basis for wealth creation and power. The opportunity for wealth creation is shown to have been instrumental in the construction of the stone tower windmill.

The grant of Henry VIII (*circa* 1545) to Augustine de Augustine, physician to the monarch and Cardinal Wolsey, gained in exchange for a payment to the monarch the Wenlock manor and he became the first lay impropriator.[37] This included 'the house and site of Wenlock Priory, its buildings, orchards fields [named in the grant] and the woods of Shirlett, Farley and Homer...there was in addition, a watermill.'[38]

This would probably be the demesne mill at the Great Pool – see Appendix 3, entry date 1536–7, p. 82.

A later grant document dated 23 Feb. 42 Elizabeth I (1600)[39] identified two estate mills, referred to as Masons Myll and the Greenemill. Masons Myll, possibly the earlier mill, was a paper mill sited at the fisheries in the area known as Pouldame – see Appendix 4, Item i) Extract p. 3 (p. 87) and Item ii) Extract 1) (p. 88). The Greenemill is likely to have been the corn mill located at the Downs. This mill was later referred to as the Downs or the Wenlock or Town's mill.

An original indenture document of Charles I (1639–40)[40] reveals that Dame Ursula Bertie entered in to a 'bargain and sell' transaction relating to the site of Great Wenlock whereby Sir Thomas Lawley of Twickenham became landlord, for a fee, for a specified term. As Sir Thomas died before the term expired, ownership of the estate reverted back to Dame Ursula in 1646 – see Appendix 2, p. 76. The indenture document also includes a reference to 'one pasture ground called *The Further Downes* then or late in the tenure of John Mason And the paper mill and two other mills called the corn mills then or late also in the occupation of the said John Mason...' This tends to imply that a corn mill existed in the area covered by the Downs Farm, the Windmill Hill and the Standhills prior to construction of the stone tower windmill. Whilst no references have yet been accessed indicating that a further mill was sited in an area immediately adjoining the Windmill Hill, W F Mumford, however, in his book dated 1977 referred to 'a disused mill to the left when viewed from the Lady Chapel' – this would be in the vicinity of the Standhills!

An indenture document dated 15 Charles II (1663/4)[41] includes a reference to 'the paper mill and two other mills called the corn mills then or late in the occupation of the said John Mason'. This second corn mill referred to in the 1663/4 indenture document would no doubt have been the stone tower windmill sited in the Windmill Hill field which was in the ownership of Dame Ursula Bertie (née Lawley).

The Lawley family, having previously acquired an estate in Wenlock in 1471, enhanced their land holdings when Thomas and Richard Lawley purchased the site and demesne land from Augustine in the same year that he acquired it from Henry VIII.[42]

The Prior's Lodging then became the Wenlock manor house and the Lawley family became the major landowners and lessors.

The rise of the Bertie family referred to previously on p. 12 continued. The marriage in 1625 of Ursula, daughter of Sir Edward Lawley, to Sir Roger Bertie, KB of the Ancaster family achieved an interest in the Wenlock estate. The incidence of local land and property transfers into tenancies then increased. Following the death of Sir Roger Bertie, KB in 1634, Ursula, the lady of the manor, married Sir George Penruddocke (b. *c.*1604, d. 1664) in 1646. Sir George already had estates in Cheshire, Wiltshire, Middlesex, Essex and Staffordshire. He was the son of Sir Thomas Penruddocke of Hale (d. after 1635) and Susan Watson of Kent (d. after 1614).

The family became divided into the Penruddockes of Hale (Hampshire) and the Penruddockes of Compton Chamberlayne (Wiltshire). The Hale family line became extinct following the death, without issue, of Charles, Edward and George of Chalk.

In 1646 [Sir] George Penruddocke, the lady of the manor's husband settled the corn tithes of Much Wenlock township on the living, augmenting it by £40.

Following the death of Dame Ursula Penruddocke in 1681 the Wenlock estate passed to Robert Bertie (*dsp* 1699), the son of her first marriage. Subsequent to the death of Robert the estate then passed to Thomas Gage. Thomas, 1st Viscount Gage, Bt. was the son of Elizabeth, daughter of Sir George Penruddocke and Dame Ursula (née Lawley), and Joseph Gage of Sherborne Castle.

The Gage family, a wealthy family with a long history of property acquisitions including estates in Gloucestershire, Monmouthshire, Herefordshire, Oxfordshire and Shropshire, had an apparent interest in purchasing extensive areas of woodland as well as being heavily involved in the early development of the copper and iron industry. The Gage family's involvement in copper- and ironworks was centred on the Hall family estate of High Meadow (Glos.) and the woodlands of the Forest of Dean.

An article referring to Sir Basil Brooke (1576–1646) of Madeley Court, Shropshire notes that 'about 1615 he obtained an interest in a patent for making steel by the cementation process'.[43] He also had business interests in the Forest of Dean when he became part-owner of two furnaces and a forge of the King's (of the Crown) ironworks. It is considered that he was also instrumental in the construction of a 'typical blast furnace' at Ironbridge, Shropshire, *c.*1638.

R Jenkins[44] in his paper referring to the ironworks in the Forest of Dean states: 'The iron seems to have had a good reputation, at any rate in the latter half of the 17th century.'

A paper by R Hayman[45] provides a comprehensive review of developments in the Shropshire iron industry *c.*1600–1900 and refers to the role of Richard Reynolds in the development of the iron industry at Coalbrookdale.

Wenlock's economy was briefly enhanced through increased exploitation of the land for stone quarrying, for timber sales as well as for coal and iron ore mining. G Williams[46] presents a comprehensive history of limestone quarrying in and around Much Wenlock. In discussing the background to limestone quarrying in Wenlock he states:

> In the early days the quarries...were small and worked in a primitive way. Often people combined other occupations such as cow keeping and beer selling, with quarrying and lime burning.

As coal and iron-ore mining in and around Wenlock increased, the use of charcoal in the iron smelting process was being superseded by using 'coking' coal. Coal could be more easily transported to the foundry and contained less contaminants. Abraham Darby further promoted the Industrial Revolution by patenting the successful casting of iron in sand moulds by 1710.

In 1714 Sir John Wynn of Gwydir purchased the estate from Viscount Gage and then left it to his cousin Sir Watkin Williams Wynn of Wynnstay in 1719. It then proceeded to pass, via other kinsmen, to its present owner.

The selection of previously published material of both a social and technical content, relevant to the period from Domesday to the destruction of the windmill in 1850 is included in Chapter 3 Secondary Source Material.

Reference is made to the technical developments and financial requirements essential for the construction of the estate's windmill to supplement rather than supersede the earlier watermills.

Results of the structural survey of Wenlock stone tower are presented in both text and diagrammatic form in Chapter 4.

The material included as Appendices 1 and 2 respectively presents 1) a review of the changes in ownership of the Windmill Hill site post-Domesday to the present owners, and 2) a summary highlighting the family interrelationships of site owners covering the perceived period of operation of the windmill, namely mid seventeenth to mid nineteenth century, the period in which milling of grain became a priority for both the landowners and the community in general.

Appendix 3 contains a record of known local millers operating in the town and parish during the sixteenth to mid-nineteenth century and attempts to establish which mill or mills they operated and the dates on which they were operating them.

The period during which they held their tenancies of the mills has not been established.

Appendix 4 presents extracts from a copy of the original document 'Survey of the Manor of Much Wenlock *c.*1700'[47] and provides an insight into the social and economic structure of a small rural environment in the seventeenth century. Reference to the complete, original document reveals a comprehensive description of the range and type of landlord's tenancy agreements and their durations.

The mills have been shown to be a major influence on local economic and political developments from feudalism through to capitalism and early industrialisation.

A consequence of the changes in land management, population densities and market forces led to the demand for a mill capable of providing a greater and more consistent output capability than the existing watermills.

The financial returns of the estate's watermills were continuing to diminish.

The early wooden-structured vertical windmills provided an opportunity for supplementing the output from watermills.

Throughout the fourteenth century, windmills capable of providing a greater output to satisfy the increasing population were being introduced, bringing further financial benefit to the mill owner whilst the feudal 'soke' laws, laws stating that the lord's mill had to be used by all tenants and freeholders, ensured a regular income to the lord well into the nineteenth century.

The earliest known reference to 'Wyndmulnehull' in Much Wenlock is a record in the 1321 Court Roll of Wenlock Priory.[48] Whilst this may imply that a windmill was sited on the 'hull' (hill), there are no known records that substantiate it. If a windmill did exist it would undoubtedly have been of wood construction and either a post mill or a smock mill, and possibly within view of the Lady Chapel.

The mid seventeenth century witnessed a period of increased wealth for some major landowners as land was dispensed by the Crown to selected persons, generally existing lords of the manor, in appreciation of their services to the monarchy. There were, however, many major landowners that suffered financial hardships as a result of enforced changes in landownership, for various reasons, during the mid seventeenth-century Civil Wars (1641–51). The demand to provide finance, manpower and livestock (horses) for the monarch's cause had an effect on the lord's wellbeing.

Joan Thirsk and H P R Finberg[49] and Ronald H Fritze and William B Robison[50] amongst others discuss the changing financial environment experienced during the seventeenth and eighteenth centuries.

Greater efficiencies in agricultural production and the use of advances in innovative 'new' materials provided the opportunity for major landowners to increase their riches as the demand for agricultural output grew.

The demand for increased and more regular supplies of milled grain to meet the needs of an expanding population, and the pursuit of changes from a feudal economy to a capitalist economy, would have been a financially attractive investment for the already wealthy landowners.

The produce from tenants and other, small, independent landowners would also have had to be milled at the lord's mill, which again raised income for the lord of the manor.

The structural survey included as Chapter 4 provides extensive technical detail of the Grade II-listed stone tower prior to commencement of preservation, in text and diagrammatic form, and reveals a series of interesting features.

Alternative opinions to those of the author suggest that the original physical height of the tower could have been less than the current height of 9 m – by approximately 2 m, i.e. to the top of the batter.

However, any extension to the height of the tower after original construction and during the period of operation would have incurred a significantly difficult and very expensive refit of milling machinery. A complete reconfiguration of all of the main and auxiliary plant items would have been necessary and possibly the main beam locations, most of which were built into the stonework as the tower was constructed. The constantly changing and uncertain economic climate of the period would have rendered such action financially unattractive.

Construction detail of the stonework at the top of the batter also tends to dispel the view that an extension of the tower took place whilst the mill was an operational unit. The coping-stones at the present height (9 m) are 'dressed' on their top outer edge and sized exactly to match the wall thickness, thus providing a suitable base upon which a curb could have been secured.

S Freese[51] states: 'In brick or stone built tower-mills (the) curb is secured by four or more very long and substantial stay bolts reaching down to 15 ft into the brickwork, which may have to be chopped away to get at the bolts if the curb ever needs renewing.' During resetting (2006) of the coping-stones around the tower top no indications of a curb attachment, as described by Freese, were apparent. Neither are there any signs lower down the internal surface of the tower where the end of stay bolts could be accessed.

Equally, the line of stonework, internally and externally, at the lower level of 7 m, does not appear to match, and therefore would not be readily suitable for carrying a tower cap assembly.

A mortar analysis at selected heights within the tower may ultimately reveal whether or not the building is of two separate periods!

V Buteux *et al.*[52] refer to buildings up to the eighteenth century containing local rubblestone for use as a filling between the inner and outer walls. The windmill tower has rubblestone filling throughout its height.

The rock quarry, Standhill (626004), to which G Williams refers, and Foxall defines as an area of fields where stone was quarried, '[may have provided] the building stone used in the construction of the Great Church and other prominent and important buildings in Wenlock [or the stone may have been] from the nearby Shadwell Quarry.' R Murchinson, an eminent geologist,[53] described the Standhill Rock as a massive reef-knoll, the limestone then being better known as 'Shropshire Marble'.[54]

In Chapter 4 Structural Survey Data reference is made to the internal wall surface towards the top of the tower identifying a series of beam pockets and elongated apertures built into the stonework – each set being located above the suggested original 7 m height of the tower. There is an obvious symmetry in the location of these, as yet, unexplained beam pocket positions, an example of which is shown in the photograph on p. 48, especially when viewed in relation to the two major high-level beams that traverse the building: see Chapter 4, diagram on p. 38.

Whilst the author's interpretation of the function of the nine and five beam pockets, along with the two crossbeams, has been previously

Photograph of beam pockets and elongated apertures.

indicated, efforts to firmly establish the function of these construction features will continue.

The professional view of Adam Marriott is that, in common with most early tower mills, the *curb* on which the *cap* rotated consisted of a wooden ring beam, usually in eight or more segments, having vertical uprights that were mortise-and-tenon-jointed into the underside.

Timbers set into the nine beam pockets as shown in Figure 3, p. 37 could have carried the vertical uprights to which Marriot refers. Apparently there are extreme occasions of this type of fixing with the verticals also jointed into the upper floor crossbeams.

The two crossbeams situated at high level, replaced in 2007, one of which is shown in the photograph on p. 49, could have served the purpose described above and also carried the floor level at 7.7 m (25.26 ft).

The lack of other observable features normally associated with a rotating cap on early tower mills, for example anchor posts projecting from the tower outer wall at intervals around the tower at low level, where a manually operated tail-pole could be fixed by the miller, or signs of a 'cartwheel track and tail-pole circle' around the mill may support the potential of a 'fixed' cap design.

Fixed cap designs were, apparently, a feature of early continental windmills, for example in the Netherlands *c.*1450 onwards. The Berties would have been familiar with such designs.

The Moidrey windmill cap is attached to a timber 'tail-pole' of approximately 150 mm × 200 mm (6 in. × 8 in.) and in the order of 6 m (20 ft) in length which projects downwards to approximately 1.5 m

A new high-level beam in position and an area of replaced coping-stones.

A typical French windmill, located at Moulin de Moidrey, Normandy, may provide the solution to the Wenlock tower cap arrangement.

(5 ft) above ground level and at a distance of 4.5 m (15 ft) from the base of the tower wall.

The photograph below shows the lower end of the tail-pole where there are two sturdy shafts of identical dimension, both secured by hinges either side of the tail-pole.

When the sails are winded the shafts are embedded into the ground to present a 'crutch' formation to lock the sails in position. To rotate the cap the miller raises both hinged shafts and secures them to the

The windmill at Moidrey, Normandy, showing the tail-pole.

The lower section of the Moidrey windmill tail-pole (2009).

main tail-pole. Having 'walked' the tail-pole to its desired position he then lowers the hinged shafts to ground to lock the sails either in or out of the prevailing wind.

Such a facility may have existed for rotating the cap on the Wenlock mill or, alternatively, the arrangement could have been similar in construction to that presented by Richard L Hill[55] when referring to a mill at Zeddam (Holland): 'There are now two wooden winches inside the *cap* which engage with wooden gearing around the *curb*.'

He continues with a reference to some Dutch drainage mills where the cap contained a winch with anchor points on the (inner) wall. Could the five elongated pockets in the wall, see Appendix 1, figures 1, 2 and 3, be anchor points for a winch within the cap?

The Bertie family would have been familiar with drainage mills as the Dutch engineer Sir Cornelius Vermuyden (b. 1590, d. 1647) introduced land reclamation methods to Britain. Vermuyden's initial involvement was to drain the Lincolnshire Fens at the same time as the Berties were given the task of draining a specific area of the Fens. Though the task was partly financed by the Berties they were, however, handsomely recompensed by the king with a grant of 24,000 acres of the cleared land.

Confirmation of the original *cap* arrangement for the Wenlock mill remains a subject for further research. However, it is unlikely that the *cap* would be of similar construction to other seventeenth- and eighteenth-century tower mills, namely wooden boat-shaped caps of appropriate physical dimension.

Sir Banister Fletcher[56] states: 'This would not have been unusual as local differences in design and construction were much affected by the peculiar organisation of the building trade during the sixteenth and nineteenth century. Masons, carpenters and others were contracted for a series of masters.'

R J De Little[57] provides an insight into caps for Shropshire mills: 'The tower of a very old mill at Gayton (Cheshire) is very short but strong, and is built from large red stone blocks. The cap of this mill is typical of Cheshire and Shropshire Mills.' However, R Wailes[58] states, 'Not only do caps vary in size and shape, but the cap bases vary considerably in construction and in nomenclature according to local practice.' He continues, 'Caps were usually typical of the areas in which the mills stood...The boat shaped caps of the north-west varied too in Lancashire, Cheshire and Anglesey.'

Whilst the technical survey observations presented above do not clearly support the prospect of a moveable cap, the installation of a 'fixed cap' mill would have significantly restricted the mill output, possibly rendering it incapable of meeting the continually increased demand for milled grain. It would also have been a very limited financial investment for the mill owner!

This photograph shows the cap design of Gayton windmill (Cheshire).

Whether the *cap* of the Wenlock mill was fixed or could be rotated remains a matter of conjecture. However, a facility similar to that of the tower at Moulin de Moidrey, Normandy, presented on p. 50, would be feasible, especially if it were constructed in a similar arrangement to that shown in Chapter 4, Figures 1, 2 and 3.

A further debatable issue is the purpose of the two 'chimney' or 'ventilation' shafts that exit at high level. One of the exits is shown in the lower photograph on page 31. The two internal 'chimney' or 'ventilation' shafts in the Much Wenlock mill are diametrically opposite each other located in the first (*stone*) floor area. Fireplaces in mills were generally situated at ground floor level and invariably only one per mill, although research, by others, shows that some mills had two fireplaces, but not specifically at first floor level.

M Watts[59] draws attention to the 'late medieval(?) windmill' at Tidenham, Gloucestershire as having two diametrically opposite doorways and a fireplace built into the wall at ground floor level in the north-east quadrant!

The four areas of red brick present in the external stonework of the tower at high level, one of which is shown in the photograph on p. 31, would appear to be 'in-fills' at a date after the original construction, possibly when the mill ceased operation.

When viewed from inside the tower it is clear from the stonework construction detail that the two major beams, referred to in the Structural Survey Data, at second floor level, had passed through the tower wall at the 'bricked infill' locations. The reason for protrusion of these two parallel beams through the external wall of the tower has yet to be ascertained.

Evidence based on the photograph of 1867 (p. 74) suggests that the original tower profile had not changed since its construction. The recently removed crenellations and the existing red-bricked infills are not apparent on this photograph.

A possible reason for the four bricked-up apertures could be to facilitate ease of removal of the two original beams once the mill had ceased operation, though the need to pass the beams through each of the four 'bricked-up' areas is considered to be an unlikely requirement since each of the beams could have been passed through a single aperture per beam.

It is also conceivable that these beams would have been severely damaged by the fire that contributed to the mill ceasing operation in 1850.

The introduction of two windows into an extended tower height, 2 m above the batter, subsequent to the 1850 lightning strike, would have been an unnecessary expenditure for an otherwise redundant structure, yet a necessary one for the original tower height. Inspection of the photograph of 1867 does not support an extended tower height either before or after the fire of 1850. The photograph also shows that dressed coping-stones were removed from the original tower top and used to top the added crenellations; therefore the crenellations that adorned the top of the tower subsequent to 1867 would appear to have been purely for aesthetic purposes.

Based on the existing physical size of the tower it is speculated by the author that the *sails* would have been a maximum of 10.4 m diameter on a *windshaft* at 10 deg. inclination. A C Norman[60] suggests the Wenlock mill would have had common sails (i.e. cloth on frames rather than the later available shuttered sails) with hand winding from an external wheel or tail-pole from the cap – see Moidrey photograph by author (p. 50).

The *brake wheel* and *brake* assembly would have been a maximum of 2.7 m diameter with the *wallower* having a diameter of 1.3 m. A compatible *great spur wheel* would be 1.4 m in diameter and each pair of *stones* being 1.2 m in diameter.

The main, central *shaft* would be a maximum of 6 m in length and, according to Marriot, provides for an *underdriven* mill, as were other Shropshire mills.

A conjectural reconstruction drawing, prepared by G Hughes[61], based on information provided by the author, reflects an *overdriven* mill.

The following schematic representations show both *underdriven* and *overdriven* arrangements.

Much Wenlock Windmill

A schematic representation showing a possible basic configuration of major equipment installed in an over-driven mill. (not to scale) Dimensions in metres.

Structural dimensions, excluding cap, are as measured. Internal mechanism dimensions are assumed.

Key: Sails @ 10.4m Ø

a) Breakwheel + Brake (max 2.7m Ø)
b) Windshaft @ 10° inclination
c) Wallower @ 1.3m Ø (0.3m deep)
d) 9 off pockets (0.18 x 0.15 x 0.23m)
e) 2 off oak beams in-situ (4.15 x 0.15 x 0.23m)
f) 5 off recesses (0.46 x 0.18 x 0.23m)
g) Great spur wheel (max 1.4m Ø)
h) Reefing Gantry
i) 2 off beams (7.3 x 0.32 x 0.32m)
j) 2 off stones (max 1.2m Ø)
k) 2 off chimney / ventilation shafts

CL

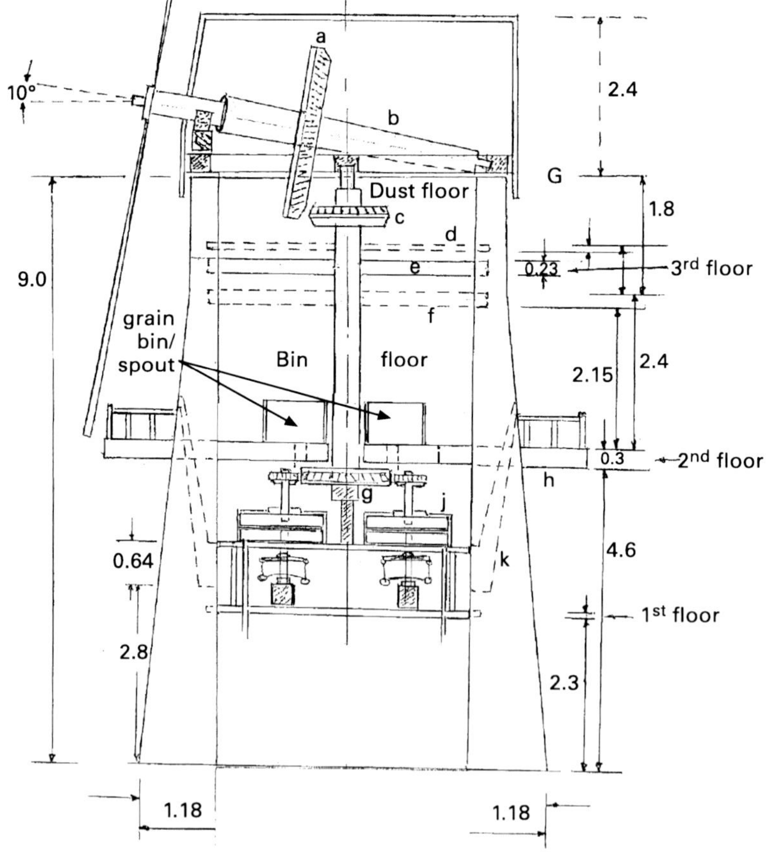

Over Driven

(not to scale)

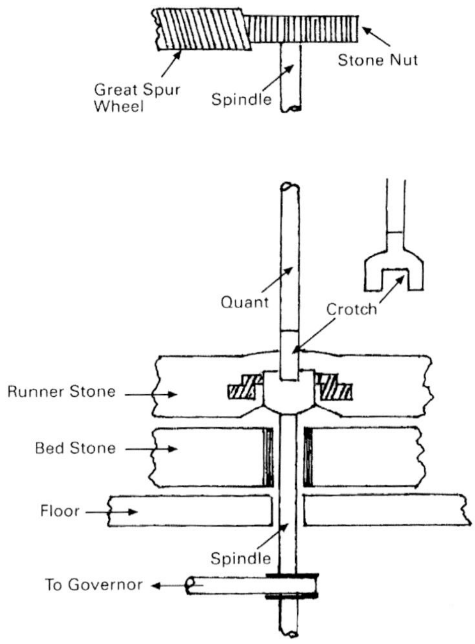

The schematic representation above, based on the survey data, depicts a possible basic *overdriven* arrangement of major milling equipment in the Much Wenlock stone tower.

The schematic representation overleaf, based on the survey data, depicts a possible basic *underdriven* arrangement of major milling equipment in the Much Wenlock stone tower.

Though the debate, by others, regarding the original height of the tower may continue (July 2009), the evidence presented previously in this book, namely the location of the high-level crossbeams and the series of large beam pockets – see photograph on p. 49 and in schematic form in Chapter 4 – would support the view that the original height of the tower was 9 m as recorded in the Structural Survey.

To introduce the number of significantly large beams in an otherwise obsolete structure subsequent to the destruction of the mill, dress all the coping-stones and insert two windows that provide limited views of the surrounding landscape, would not present a financially viable activity.

Much Wenlock Windmill

A schematic representation showing a possible basic configuration of major equipment installed in an under-driven mill. (not to scale) Dimensions in metres.

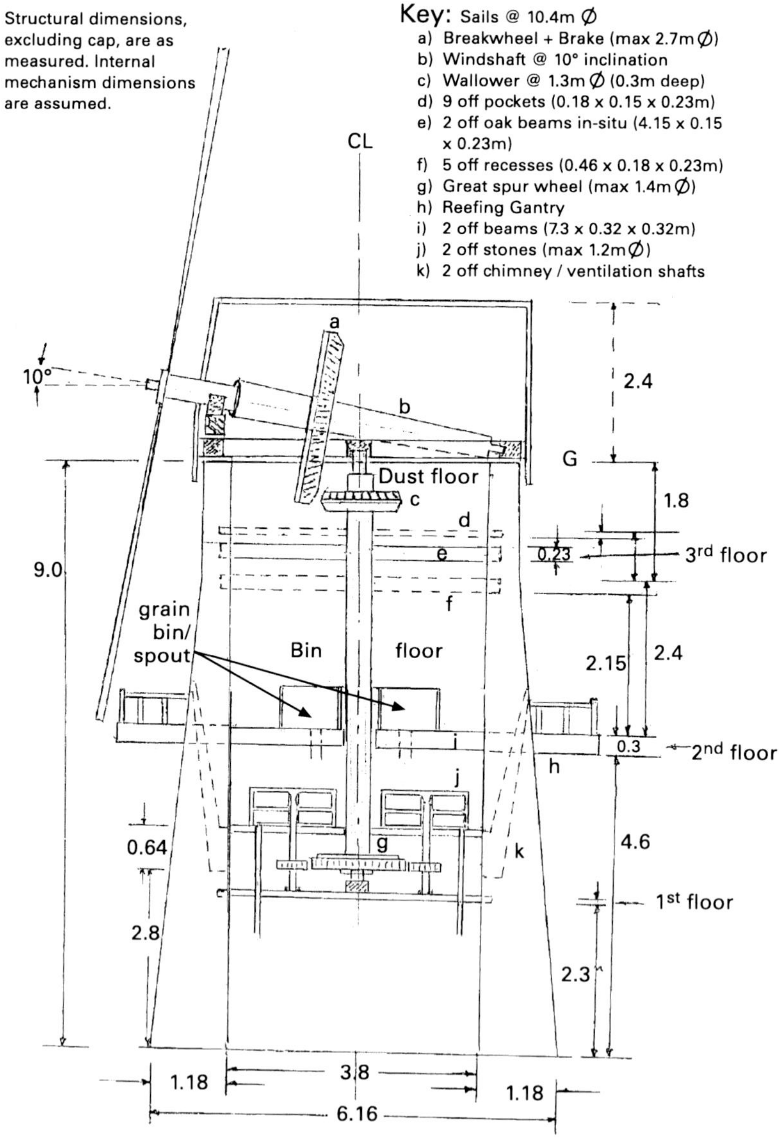

Under Driven

(not to scale)

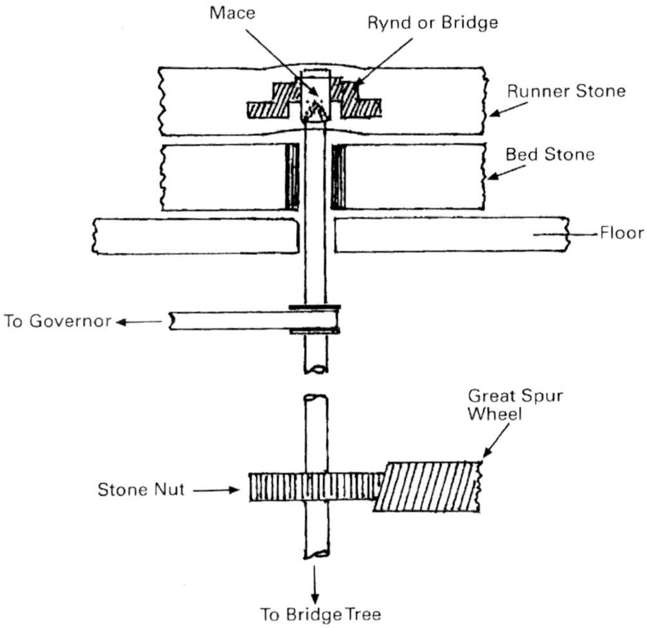

Freese notes that cloth sails were introduced in 1300 and fixed mill sails always pointed into the prevailing wind. By 1588 the present type of brake assembly was in use and both brick and stone towers were in general use.

Though the essential ancillary items required for completing the milling process and their likely locations within the Wenlock tower have not been established, it is likely that the type and range of ancillary items would have been basically similar to the equipment in the earlier water- and post mills but not as sophisticated as those referred to by Freese and Hill. Speculation of a basic internal configuration by the author is included below.

Freese and Hill provide a series of significant dates from the mid eighteenth century for the introduction of milling machinery developments:

> By 1745 the fantail assembly was being used for automatically facing the sails into the prevailing winds.
> Cast-iron wheels were being installed by 1752 and within eight years the first iron-toothed gears were cast and introduced into windmills along with iron shafts.

Freese reflects that Thomas Mead patented the centrifugal governor for mill stone speed control.
Hill states that by 1800 head and tail layouts became popular which coincided with the introduction of automatic sail control.

These developments enabled the introduction of larger towers with extra stones that could be driven via the stone nuts on either side of the great spur wheel. The centrifugal bolter was introduced by 1850.

The physical location of some of the ancillary items installed is speculated upon, based on an interpretation of the function of a specific section of internal stonework that is shown in diagrammatic form on p. 33. The position of the section relative to the south-facing doorway and at a height of 5.38 m above floor level may have been a part of the facility for anchoring the sack hoist assembly which may have been driven, via a horizontal shaft, off the great spur wheel. If this were the case then the position of the trap doors, through which the sacks would have passed when raised to the bin floor, may be established and the likely positions of the stairways identified.

The grain would presumably have been received at the south-westerly orientated door with the meal being dispatched at the north-easterly door.

It is likely that the *sieve* or *bolter,* an early type of flour-dresser device used for separation and sizing the flour into different grades was, typically, a circular wooden frame covered by a fabric sleeve and placed on an incline. The fabric sleeve would have been of fine mesh at the top, the entrance of the meal, with an increasing size of mesh towards the bottom of the incline.

The unit could have been rotated via a belt drive from the main, or an auxiliary, shaft with a 'rapping' arrangement designed to segregate the differing sizes of milled grain.

Though *sieves* or *bolters* were introduced in 1614 it was not until 1765 that a more sophisticated device, having three grading facilities, was patented. The *centrifugal bolter* was not available until 1850. The *centrifugal bolter* would not have been fitted retrospectively in the Wenlock mill.

A *governor* and *tentering screw* could have been located in the ground floor area for convenient access. The *governor,* a device for automatically maintaining the correct gap between the mill stones, was likely to have been belt-driven from the *stone spindle* which supported the *runner,* or top rotating *stone.*

The following photographs on p. 60 show the detail of a millstone situated adjacent to Downs Mill (Much Wenlock).

Mr Tim Booth[62] (Midland Wind and Water Mills Group) provides an interpretation, based on the photographs presented to him by the author, of the type and application of each millstone. The Downs Mill stone is a peak (*millstone grit)* stone, made as a *bedstone* with a *square eye* and a cast-iron *neck box*. The *neck box* held the bearing which positioned the *stone spindle* driving the *runner stone*. The *runner stone* would have rotated clockwise. The *stone* is typically nineteenth century and would have been used for grinding animal feed.

The *stone* at Bradley Mill is rather different. The photographs on page 61 appears to show many large quartz pebbles in the *stone* which could mean that it is a Welsh stone from the Wye valley. There are no obvious *rind chases* (slots), so it was a *bedstone*. Again, the *runner stone* would have turned clockwise. Its small size, domed back and the style of dressing all suggest that is a very old stone, possibly seventeenth century, but could be earlier. Welsh stones were often used for flour milling.

The physical location of the water course to the Bradley millpond, the position of the output chute and sluice valve from the pond and the outfall duct that discharge into the adjacent Farley Brook reflect an early horizontal mill arrangement.

The schematic representations on pages 54 and 56 present the physical arrangement of millstones for an *over-* and *underdriven* mill. It is concluded that both the Downs and Bradley mills were underdriven arrangements.

It will be noted that the *rind (rynd)* or *bridge* – a metal bar cemented into the *eye* of the *runner stone* – acts as a bearing for the *spindle*.

The *quant*, a four-sided shaft from the *stone nut* to *mace*, appears only on *overdriven stones*.

The *governor* (and the *tentering screw*) in the schematic representations on pages 55 and 57 would probably have been located within the first floor area. The *tentering screw* enabled the miller to manually adjust the gap between the *runner* and *fixed* bottom *stone* for determining the quality of the finished *meal*.

The more advanced *centrifugal governors* for *millstones* were not in use until the late 1700s. It is therefore unlikely that either of these features, the *three grading sieve* or *bolter* and the *centrifugal governor*, would have been fitted retrospectively in the Wenlock mill.

The position of the opening in the tower wall, above and to the side of the southerly-facing doorway, having an external quoin of orange/red brickwork (see photograph on p. 32), could also support the view that the stairway was located in this area. The internal construction of the opening is considerably larger than the external opening and capable of providing a wide-angled view of the landscape for the miller.

Existence of the local windmill would have had a significant role in forming the social and economic environment of Wenlock township for, as Seaby and Smith identified (Table 2.4: Windmills in Shropshire of which the towers remain[63]), optional alternative milling facilities locally were few and far between.

The stone at Downs Mill has an overall diameter of 1.219 m (4 ft).

Photograph showing the 21.6 × 21.6 cm (8.5 × 8.5 in,) centre.

The stone at Bradley Mill is approximately 0.914 m (3 ft) overall diameter. The centre hole is approx. 80 mm (3.5 in.) diameter.

This shows the back of the stone with a depth at the centre approx. 80 mm (3.5 in.) tapering to the outer edge to approx. 50 mm (2 in.)

The logistics of transporting grain long distances, often over difficult terrain using dubious forms of transport, would have incurred higher milling costs in terms of time and labour and at the same time reduced valuable income to the lord.

The prime justification for constructing the stone tower would, therefore, appear to have been one of securing increased wealth for the owner, mainly as a result of the evolving national and local socio-economic climate of the sixteenth and early seventeenth century. The mill would have provided the landlord with a more sustainable, and therefore profitable, opportunity to mill the increased volumes of grain produced on his greater land mass. The mill capacity would, presumably, meet the need of an expanding population, at the same time as securing additional regular income from lesser landowners through higher-value property and land leases.

The application of the Soke Laws that deemed all demesne grain had to be milled at the landlord's mill would also have had to be catered for.

Anecdotal material supports a view that the Lawley/Bertie family had adequate funds available for building a stone tower windmill. Richard Lawley, having bought the land of Callaughton from the Crown in 1543, proceeded to build a property known as Spoonhill House in which he lived until his death in 1569. The estate remained in the family until the mid nineteenth century.

The Lawley family would have had access to a combination of local craftsmen, including stonemasons, carpenters, wheelwrights and blacksmiths.

Descendants of these earlier tradespeople who built Spoonhill House, or other local skilled journeymen, could, in conjunction with an experienced miller, have been involved in the construction of the stone tower windmill.

The general sparsity of available estate records of expenditure specifically on labour and material for the mill construction and maintenance repairs could be attributed to the fact that the majority of goods and services would have been provided 'in-house' with costs allocated to other diverse accounts. However, 'bought-in' goods and services, including millstones, iron components and sails cloth would, normally, have been recorded in specific expenditure accounts.

Though the Lawley/Bertie family are recorded as owners of the Windmill Hill site during the mid seventeenth century there are no definitive records noting ownership of the parcel of land upon which the tower was built.

As noted earlier, on the Foxall map of 1847 – see p. 23 – the Windmill Hill site was recorded as plot 259 with the windmill tower as plot 260, basically 'a plot within a plot', having a footprint of 30¼ square yards (one perch). This may imply that the tower was built on the landlord's property, funded by the landlord but was in tenure or occupation of others.

One particular local family, the Masons, were prominent tenants of the Berties throughout the seventeenth century. The extent of their tenures of parcels of land would have raised their status quite comfortably beyond the earlier feudal category known as villeins to that of a 'free tenant' – the wealthier class of peasant – where they would have occupied a unique place in medieval hierarchy, often benefiting from low rents and subjected to fewer laws and ties than villeins.

Entries in the original Indenture Documents, 1639/40 and 1663, identify John Mason as miller of a paper mill and two other mills called the Downs mills. The inscription date of 1655, located by the author in September 2009 within the inner wall of the stone tower, at a depth of 0.3 m (14 in.), could only have been inserted during construction of the tower, as access to the location subsequent to construction would have been impossible.

The Much Wenlock windmill is, therefore, considered to be one of the early versions of a stone tower mill, built and operational during 1655/7.

The last will and testament of Richard Coundley senior, carpenter, dated 1685, considered to be the miller at the windmill subsequent to John Mason, notes: 'I assigne and set over all right, title, interest

The inscription date of 1655 (see also diagram on page 33), located by the author in September 2009, is embedded within the tower wall at a depth of 0.3 m (14 in.) and could only have been inserted during construction of the tower, as access to the location subsequent to construction would have been impossible.

This photograph shows the later date of 1657, which is readily accessible and would have been inscribed on the inner wall surface finish when the mill became operable. The initials FM accompanying the inscribed date of 1657 could conceivably be that of Fran Mason, a relative of John Mason, the first recorded miller at the windmill – see Appendix 3, p. 78. Fran Mason is recorded as having a lease from Dame Ursula Bertie dated 1665 (see Appendix 1, p. 70).

I have in the mills I now hold of my landlord Esquire Bertie, And to have and to hold the said mills for the years yet to run'.

As there were only two watermills serving the priory at the time of the dissolution, namely the Downs mill and the Paper mill – the Grene Myll at Poole Dam – it could, therefore, be assumed that the second corn mill referred too was an earlier mill, perhaps a horse mill at Downs mill.

Interestingly, the inventory of Richard Coundley's goods and chattels dated 15 June 1686 includes a series of records:

> Implements and tooles belonging to Carpenters trade or Millwrights with mill-picks to the value of 00 10 00.
> Three Horses att. to the value of 08 10 00
> One carte and gears, hackney saddle, packsaddle and Pads, for the mill-horses att. to the value of 01 00 00
> Two spinning wheels to the value of 00 01 06
> Muck or manure about the Mills to the value of 00 07 00.

Further research, with redefined objectives, could possibly identify the range, size and configuration of all relevant, originally installed, ancillary equipment. The milling equipment would have been predominantly of wood construction which may have been supplemented by a limited number of iron components. It is possible that the iron components could have been produced locally at the Shirlett forge.

As the windmill is situated in close proximity to Coalbrookdale, the area where developments in the process of smelting iron were taking place at the time the windmill was under construction, some of the products from the early furnaces of Sir Basil Brooke and Abraham Darby may also have been incorporated into the windmill.

Records indicate that ironwork was purchased from 'Coal Brook Dale for the corn mill' in 1858, presumably for the Downs watermill, which was still in operation.

If the windmill had included iron components from the Coalbrookdale foundries, it would have played a part in the start of the Industrial Revolution.

Whilst a number of references are made to the ownership, and tenancies, of the Windmill Hill site, as yet there are no known definitive records of the original owners of the stone tower windmill.

Authenticated data from a wide range of often sparse original records have been sought during pursuit of this research project. It has became abundantly clear throughout this research that little attempt had been made previously to establish the history of mill development and milling in Much Wenlock specifically and Shropshire generally. It is therefore hoped that through completion of the primary objective the secondary objectives to establish a typical type, size and configuration of the internal milling mechanism of Much Wenlock windmill can be pursued and the early history of Shropshire mills will become a subject for further investigation.

The windmill subsequent to completion of the first stage of preservation (Sept. 2009).

Appendix 1

Chronology of Site Ownership – post-dissolution of the monastery

The material presented below forms an essential part of the research into the origin of the windmill by providing an overview of the local socio-economic and political environment of Much Wenlock township subsequent to the dissolution of the monastery.

Post-dissolution of the monastery was the period when landownership became a symbol of wealth and power.

History reveals that a number of major landowners acquired parts of the monastic property immediately following the dissolution. Some of these families appear to have been speculators and/or absent landowners as parcels of land changed ownership frequently.

The following chronological presentation is primarily a summary of the family interrelationships of known major estate owners, over the period mid sixteenth century to mid nineteenth century, the period in which the windmill operated. It is during this period of landownership that the estate's original two watermills, used to serve the monks, were supplemented and ultimately superseded by the tower windmill.

Stone tower mills were more robust structures and, when sited at suitable physical locations, were capable of a greater sustainable output capability than earlier mills but, equally, required greater levels of skill and expenditure to build and maintain. Major landowners would, inevitably, have been the only source of the significant finance required.

1540: The advowson (property which may be bought or sold or given away but remains subject to civil law) of the Wenlock vicarage descended with the rectory, passing to the Crown. On the eve of the dissolution, many abbeys sold their advowsons to friends and relatives, or alternatively a resident curate was appointed.

The dissolved Wenlock priory became a ready source of building material for the town's inhabitants and many local buildings were constructed.

1545: The land area purchased from the Crown by Augustine de Augustine, the first lay impropriator, comprised approximately 850 acres of arable, pasture, meadows and woods. The watermill is considered to have been the one known as Grene Myll (Grenemill*) and was located at Downs Farm, hence the mill became known later as Downs Mill.

The Wenlock demesne mill – Masons Myll* – is recorded as being situated at the Great Pool (Pouledamme) on a tributary of Farley Brook.

Augustine sold the priory site and demesne lands to Thomas Lawley, Merchant of the Staple (d. 1559), and brother Richard of Spoonhill (d. 1569) for the sum of £1609. 6s.

Brothers Richard and Thomas also purchased Hopton and Monk Hall as one manor, but it was often referred to as two manors.

1546: Thomas Bertie of Bersted, 'Mr Bert', was appointed Captain of Hurst Castle and granted arms, thereby raising his status to that of gentleman.

1546/7: The borough was now represented in Parliament by two MPs, namely Richard and Thomas Lawley of Wenlock.

1569: Richard Lawley of Spoonhill (and ultimately of Tipton, Staffs) died and the Bourton estate passed to his son Francis (d. 1583). It then passed to his son Richard (d. 1623) and continued on through the family to 1834.

1559: Thomas Lawley of Wenlock died.

1571: The Wenlock estate house passed from Thomas Lawley's widow Beatrix Hinton (daughter of Griffin Hinton) to their eldest son Sir Thomas Lawley of Wenlock (d. 22.2.1621), who married Elizabeth Newport (the widow of his brother Francis), daughter of Sir Richard Newport of High Ercall.

The house then became known as the Much Wenlock manor house.

1576: Almoners Croft (Amners Ground) and pasture called Stanley passed from the Crown into the Lacon family who then sold the lands to Samuel Edwards.

---

*As referred to in the Grant of Queen Elizabeth (see Appendix. 4, Item i), Extract p. 3).

The almonry was sited opposite the medieval gatehouse into the precinct, on one side of which was the porter's lodge and the prison of the franchise.

1585: Sir Thomas Lawley of Wenlock, Kt. and Robert his brother (sons of Thomas and Beatrix) bought the manor from the Crown. They also bought almost the whole estate of the former service of Our Lady in the parish church. Thomas lived in the prior's lodgings.

(See also the extracts from the original transcript of the Grant from Queen Elizabeth in the section 'Historical Documents' below.)

1590: The Crown sold the advowson of the vicarage to Henry Bromley who, earlier, had inherited his father Thomas's (d. 1587) land, except for Holt Castle.

The advowson and tithes then passed to Thomas Lawley whose wife, Elizabeth, was Bromley's cousin.

1600: The Crown sold Much Wenlock manor, which was administered separately from Bourton Hundred, to Thomas and Richard Lawley who, at the same time, bought a large proportion of the estate of the former service of Our Lady in the parish church.

1601: Robert Bertie, the 14th Baron Willoughby de Eresby, pursued a distinguished military career. He was created first Earl of Lindsey on 22 November 1626 (b. 1583, d. 1642). Robert had two sons, Montague and Roger.

Through a series of high-profile marriages members of the Bertie family became peers of the realm and proceeded to serve the reigning monarchs.

1614: Sir Thomas Lawley (d. 1621), now with sole possession of the manor and a large part of the estate, was succeeded by his son Sir Edward Lawley, Kt. of Wenlock, Co. Salop (d. 1623) who married Susan Fisher (daughter of Sir Thomas Fisher, Bt. of Islington). Sir Edward had a daughter Ursula (b. 1612, d. 1681).

1621: Sir Thomas Lawley's wife was passed the advowson and tithes.

1623: Sir Edward died and the manor of Wenlock along with the rectorial tithes of Much Wenlock township of 1590 passed to his daughter Ursula, aged nine years and four months, his heir.

1630: Ursula, daughter of Sir Edward Lawley, married the Hon. Sir Roger Bertie, KB of the Ancaster family (d. 1634), second son of Robert Bertie, 1st Earl of Lindsey.

1631: The borough's charter of 1468 was reconfirmed without detriment to Sir Roger Bertie's manorial holdings (his manor, jurisdiction and privileges).

The Borough of Wenlock continued to be the largest non-county borough in England, covering 37 square miles (approx. 23,600 acres), yet with one of the lowest population density levels.

Charles I (ruled 1625–49): empowered [authorised] Sir Roger Bertie, KB and Ursula, his wife, to 'alienate [transfer] the site of the Priory of Great Wenlock to [brother] Montague Lord Willoughby and [uncle] Henry Bertie [b. 1577, d. 1655]'. The transfer ended three generations of Lawley residence at the priory.[64]

1634: The death of Sir Roger Bertie, KB was recorded as 'of such persons as made default at the musters at Stafford on 4th June last and at Lichfield this day'.[65]

1636: The Grant of Livery dated 28 September[66] headed 'Francis Lacon, son and heir of Silvan Lacon deceased, of possessions of late Silvan Lacon' refers to family land ownership in Wenlocke Magna: 'land called Le Amners in Wenlocke Magna, and all lands, leasows, etc. of late dissolved monastery of Much Wenlocke, tithes from above said Amners Ground or of the office of almoner; pastures called Stanley with apps [appurtenances], late parcel of manor of Wenlocke Magna and of monastery, held of the manor of East Greenewich, Kent, in free and common socage for fealty and annual rent of 22s'.

A further entry reveals that Almoners Lands were part of a marriage settlement of 28 May 1708 of John Lacon the younger and Jane his wife.

The Lacon family had property interests in Wenlocke Magna through the seventeenth century to, at least, the mid eighteenth century.

1639 (2 August): Mortgage by Release[67] for £1600: Dame Ursula Bertye (née Lawley) to Thomas Lawley of Twickenham esq.* – Site of Greate Wenlock Priory.

Consisting: Lands in Much Wenlock with 2 pastures lying north-eastward between the Priory House and Paper Mill. Mentions meadow called Pouledamme, pasture called Cutlers Yard, two Sandhills and 'the connyes there or upon'; meadows called Broad Meadowe (2), Bellhole, Mill Meadowe, the Broad Meadowe and Pinfold Meadowe.

---

*Sir Thomas was father of Sir Francis, Thomas and Elizabeth (see Appendix 2).

Pasture ground called Newe Leasowe, Lercroft, Hether Downs and Upper part of Ruffe Downs; mills called the Paper Mill and 2 corne mills.

Pasture called Upper and Lower Wallmers, New Leasowe and Pinfold Pasture, Further Downs, Bradley Meadowe, Waltonhill Pasture and Ruff Downs, Avenors Croft, Calve Croft; Messuages (dwelling houses with outbuildings and land assigned to their use); 102 ac. In **Windmillhill Field**, Edgefield and Shinewhead Furlonge; 24 acres in Bradley Furlonge and Knightstreetfield; 34 acres in Southfield. (Tenants named.)

1641: The baronetcy of Lawley of Spoonhill in the County of Shropshire was created in the Baronetage of England on 16 August for Thomas Lawley, who represented Wenlock in Parliament in 1625–6 and 1628–9.

1646: Sir Thomas Lawley, 1st Baronet of Spoonhill died. His son, Sir Francis Lawley, 2nd Baronet (b. *c*.1630, d. October 1696) inherited the baronetcy and the estate.

Ursula Lawley's second marriage was to Sir George Penruddocke, Kt. of Ivy Church, Wilts. (b. *c*.1604, d. 1664). Their daughter Elizabeth Penruddocke (d. 1693) married Joseph Gage of Sherborne Castle, son of Sir Thomas Gage, 2nd Baronet (d. 1654).

1651: Sir George Penruddocke, Kt. was lord of Much Wenlock.

Sir Francis Lawley of Canwell Priory, 2nd Baronet of Spoonhill was MP for Wenlock and Shropshire 1659–60 and 1661–79 and was also lord of Bourton, Callaughton, Hopton and Monk Hall.

The Lawleys proceeded thereafter to 'lease for 3 lives' some of their property in and around Much Wenlock.

1671: A Much Wenlock probate entry of 20 Nov. for Fran Mason 'Imprimis the decedts [the first deceased?] – Interest in one lease taken from Dame Ursula Bertie the first day of April in the seventeenth year of our Sovereign Lord Charles the Second. Ann. Dni. 1665.'[68]

1681: Ursula Penruddocke (née Lawley) died; the Wenlock estate was transferred from the Lawley family to the son of her first marriage, Robert Bertie (b. bef. 1634 – *dsp* 1699).

1695 (23 Dec.): Robert Bertie of the Middle Temple bequeathed the manor to Thomas Gage, 1st Viscount Gage, Bt. (b. before 1702, [Baron 1720] d. 1754), and his heirs in tail.

Thomas, the son of Joseph Gage of Sherborne Castle and Elizabeth Penruddocke (d. 1693) of Hale, daughter of Ursula Lawley and Sir George Penruddocke, married (1714) Benedicta Maria Theresa Hall (d. 1749), daughter of Henry Benedict Hall and Frances Fortesque, wealthy landowners of High Meadow, Gloucestershire.[69]

'Thomas Gage, Esq., lord of the manor of Wenlock, a Roman Catholick and during his minority Sir William Goring, Bart., a Roman Catholick was his guardian who lived very distant from the said manor.'[70]

1699: Following the death of Robert Bertie the manorial estate 'tenancies at will' (agreement between tenant and landlord – not transferable) were substituted for expiring leases.

1714: A survey of the manor was undertaken for Sir John Wynn prior to his purchasing it from Viscount Gage in 1714 by John Reynolds, possibly a kinsman of John Reynolds who held a messuage or tenement in Spittle Street called the White Hart from Robert Bertie, Esq. in September 1672.

Viscount Gage sold the manor to Sir John Wynn of Gwydir (d. 1719) – a kinsman of the Berties of Ancaster – who married Jane Evans (daughter of Eyton Evans of Watstay). Wenlock manor was one of a number of estates possessed by Sir John.

The manorial estate then comprised meadow land (1/6 of all agricultural land) and permanent pasture, including Westwood Common (a half of all agricultural land).

Wenlock manor was one of a number of estates in the possession of Sir John.

1719: Sir John Wynn of Gwydir left the manor to his cousin Sir Watkin Williams Wynn of Wynnstay (3rd Baronet 1740, d. 1749), who added the surname Wynn.

Sir Watkin Williams Wynn began to offer chattel leases (if leasehold land was dispossessed it could be recovered); many such leases were made in the late 1720s and some presumably lasted until the 1820s.

A succession of millers paid rent for the windmill and watermill to the estate.[71]

1726: The (Wenlock) estate settlement of 19 July is a settlement of what remained of the estate at that date, after it had been considerably reduced in size by systematically selling parcels of the land.[72]

1745: The parcel of land known as Almoner's Croft and Barn was bought by Thomas Mare who held it through to 1790. The parcel of land had passed from the Crown in 1576 through a succession of owners. The original land transfer had included an area of pasture known as the Stanley.

Was this the same Mayre (Mare) family recorded as millers at Masons mill of the early sixteenth century (see Appendix 3, p. 78 entries for 1534 and 1595)?

1764: Two great landowner families merged when Sir Robert Lawley, 5th Baronet of Spoonhill (b. 1736, d. 1793), whose family had held lands in Shropshire since 1471 and whose family seat was at Canwell Hall in Staffordshire, married Jane Thompson (b. 1743, d. 1816), the sister of Beilby Thompson of Escrick, Yorkshire and heiress to the Escrick estates south of the city of York.[73]

1769: Plans existed to reduce the number of farms (on the estate) in expectation of the Much Wenlock Enclosure Act of 1775.

Authenticated historical records of local enclosures covering the period 1730–1875, relating specifically to the Windmill Hill site and the windmill, have yet to be identified.

1779: The will of Sir Robert Lawley of Canwell Priory, 4th Baronet of Spoonhill (1st creation 1641) (d. 1779) (probate 1780), detailed the leasing of his land. The document also provides brief details of acreage assigned to members of his family, but does not specify where the land is situated.[74]

1790: Thomas Mare's son-in-law, Col. (later Gen.) Dudley Ackland, sold his estate to Geo. Forester.[75]

1808: As a result of the Enclosure Act the Wynn estate holdings over 25 acres fell from 16 in 1714 to nine, which increased greatly in size.

1831: The baronetcy of Lawley (1641) merged with the second creation. Robert Lawley became Baron Wenlock. The title became extinct following the death of Robert Lawley in 1834.

1848: Lord Forester now owned 194 acres of land in and around the town of Much Wenlock and continued with further purchases. By 1858 he had acquired a further 827 acres, over half of the manorial estate, from Sir Watkin Williams Wynn.

J M Gaskell bought the lordship of the manor and the rest of the estate. Much of the Forester estate in Much Wenlock was sold in the twentieth century.[76]

1858: The manor ceased descending within the Williams Wynn baronetcy when it was bought by Sir Watkin's niece's husband James Milnes Gaskell (d. 1873) of Thornes House (West Riding of Yorkshire).

The Abbey had become a decayed farmhouse but James Milnes Gaskell, followed by his son Charles G Milnes Gaskell (d. 1919), who married Lady Catherine Wallop, daughter of the Earl of Portsmouth, restored it as a gentleman's country house. Mary, the daughter of Charles and Lady Catherine Milnes Gaskell (d. 1935), married General H D O Ward and inherited the Wenlock estate. (Evelyn, the son of Charles and Lady Catherine, inherited their Wakefield estate.)

1859: The Wenlock Olympian Society Games programme refers to a note from J M Gaskell, Esq., which states that [he] '...has kindly given directions for fitting-up of the tower of the old windmill, from the summit of which an excellent view may be obtained of the Games and the surrounding countryside.'[77]

1867: The photograph taken at the annual Wenlock Olympian Games Meeting is the oldest known photograph of a sporting event.[78] The Windmill Hill site was used as a viewing platform by the spectators. The remains of the stone tower windmill, destroyed by lightning in 1850, can be seen in the background of the picture on p. 74.

1932: Both the barony and the baronetcy of Lawley became extinct.

1953: Mary Ward left the estate 'in trust' to the four sons of her niece Mary Milnes Gaskell (b. 1906, d. 1999), the daughter of Evelyn Milnes Gaskell and Lady Constance Knox, who married Lewis Motley.

1983: Louis de Wet and his wife Gabrielle Drake purchased the Abbey from the Motley family.

1996: Mr Tim Motley of Wenlock Estates said that the estate had looked at their definitive title to all the properties in the estate's ownership and found that the windmill was not included. He concluded that the estate had no claim of ownership for the windmill, although it did own Windmill Hill. (ref. Bridgnorth Journal 26.10.1996.)

The windmill tower can be seen in the background of this 1867 photograph of the annual Wenlock Olympian Games. The Windmill Hill was used as a viewing area for this sporting event.

Appendix 2

Family relationships of relevant landowners

The following notes present a résumé of Lawley/Bertie/Penruddocke and Gage families interrelationships based on material derived from a series of sources. Progression of the Lawley family members – 'of Wenlock' and 'of Spoonhill'– through to the marriages of Ursula Lawley of Wenlock to Sir Roger Bertie, KB, then to Sir George Penruddocke and on to the Gage family, is presented.

Family Relationships of relevant landowners

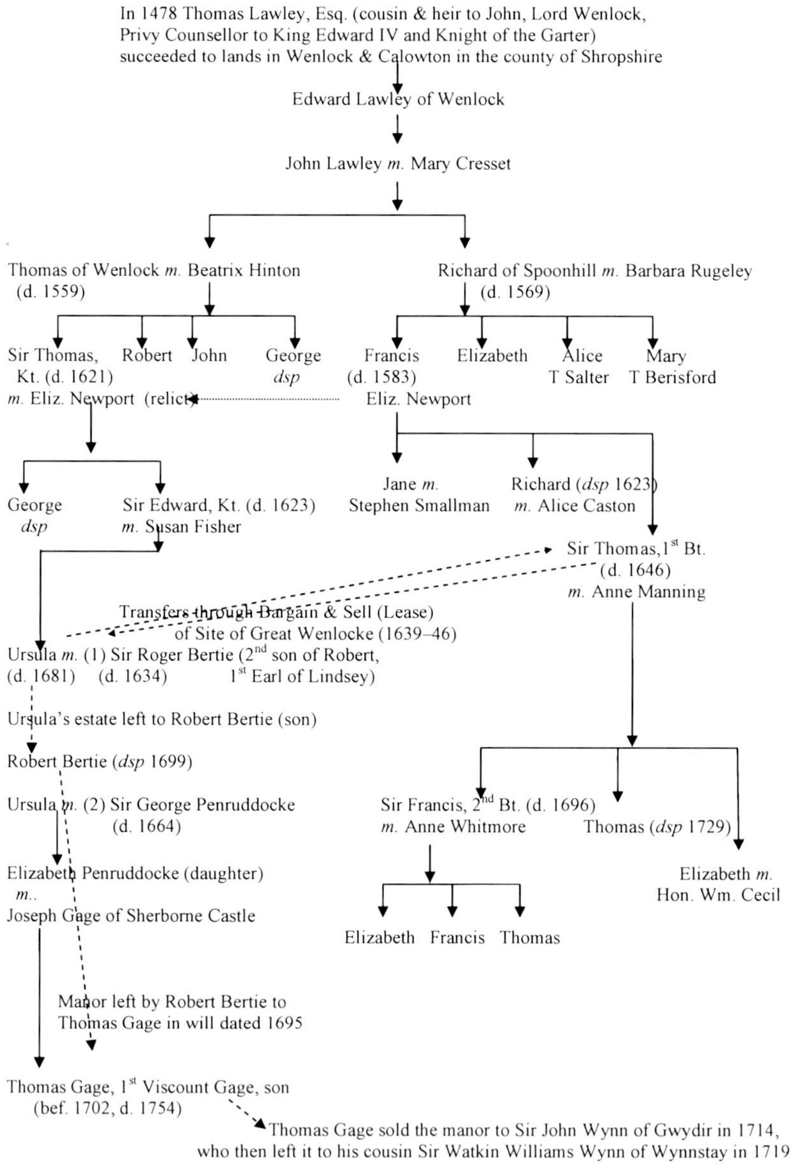

Note: The arrowed dotted lines indicate the known transfer of the estate inclusive of the Windmill Hill site, not necessarily the windmill tower.

Appendix 3

History of Milling in Much Wenlock

Previously published history of the tower includes:

- Pre-1645 built as a guard tower
- *Circa* 1622–47 may have been a malt mill
- Pre-1713 located on map as a windmill
- Pre-1750 earliest known date of remaining (windmill) tower in Shropshire, with the last date of operation *c.*1890
- 1850 windmill struck by lightning and ceased operation

The following list comprises recorded local millers identified to date (Jan 2009); the dates denote the presence of the miller in stated locations. Some confusion remains regarding precise physical location of the various mills! The table does not identify the start and end dates of occupation of the mills.

	Miller	Location	Land Owner
1534	Mayres or Mayors	Masons Myll (the Paper Mill)	Priory
1595	William More*	Greene Mill (Grenemyll)	Lawleys
"	Thomas Mare*	Masons Mill (Myll) at Pool Dam (Fish-pond)	"
1647	Edward Embre	The corn mill & the little meadow above yt	Berties[79]
"	John Gower }		
	Hugh Kinge }	The Paper mill & The Poole Dam	"
"	Joyce Watkin}		
	Jos. Cooke }	The Malt Mill	"
"	Edward Embre	The corne mill	"
1661	John Clarke	Farley Mill	Unknown
1663	William More	Enne Myll (Wynnstay 3905/2) (Greene Mill)	"
"	John Mason	Paper Mill & two Corn Mills	Berties**
1675	John Mason	Paper Mill & two Corn Mills	"
Pre-1685	Richard Coundley (senior)	Windmill & two water grist mills	"
1685	Richard Coundley (junior)	" " " " "	"
1702	Francis Selman	Paper Mill	"
1709	Ann Hancock	Paper Mill	"
1714	Richard Connley	Windmill & two water grist mills	Watkin Williams Wynn
1723	John Share (Shore)	Three Bradley (Budbach) Watermills	Unknown
"	Thomas Stevens, Gent	One " "	leased from John Share
"	Thomas Bickerton, Clothier	" " "	" " " "
"	Eldred Lancelot Lee	" " "	" " " "
1730	Joseph Hughes	Masons Mill	Berties
1750	John Windsor	Bradley Mill	Unknown
1754	John Norrey	Parish Miller (source SRO Marriage Register)	"
1759	John Clarke	" " " " "	"
"	Thomas Dodd	" " " " "	"
1760	Edward Jeffreys	" " " " "	"
1764	Edward Triston?	" " " " "	"
1770	Thomas Pillson?	" " " " "	"

Date	Name	Description	Owner
*c.*1770	Eldred Lancelot Lee relinquishes Bradley paper mill; it was 'cropped out'		
1774	Sarah Windsor assigned *two* watermills to William Jefferys		"
"	William Cooke	Town or Wenlock Miller (source SRO Baptisms Record)	"
1815	William Jeffreys	Dwons watermill and windmill (source SRO 4791/1/10)	"
"	Joseph Reynold	Farley Miller " " " "	"
1817	Richard Jeffreys	Town or Wenlock Miller " " " "	"
1817	William Milner	Farley Miller " " " "	"
1818	William Milner	Farley Miller " " " "	"
1818	Richard Jeffreys	Town or Wenlock Miller " " " "	"
1823	Richard Jeffreys	" " " " " " "	"
"	John Rogers	Farley Miller " " " "	"
1824	Richard Jeffreys sold *two* Bradley Mills to Thomas Harper & Son		
1827	" "	Bradley Miller (source SRO Baptisms Record)	
1828	John Dodd		Watkin Williams Wynn
1831	Richard Jeffreys	Town or Wenlock Miller (source SRO Baptisms Record)	"
"	Illegible	Farley Miller " " " "	"
1836	Richard Jeffreys	Town or Wenlock Miller " " " "	"
1842	Thomas Yates	Farley Miller " " " "	"
1842	John Embry	Farley Miller " " " "	"
1843	" "	" " " " " "	"
1845	" "	" " " " " "	"
1847	William Jeffreys	Windmill and Downs mill	"
1848	John Embry	Farley Miller (source SRO Baptisms Record)	"
1850	John Jones	" " " " " "	"
"	Richard Jeffreys	Town or Wenlock Miller " " " "	"
"	William Jeffreys	The Windmill	"
1851	Thomas Harper & Son		James Milnes Gaskell

*Note: The Grant document of Elizabeth I dated 1569 refers to the Greenemyll being in the tenure or occupation of William More whilst Masons Myll and the fisheries, etc. and Aumers barn and croft were in the tenure or occupation of Thomas Manne alias Mayer in the 24th year of Elizabeth's reign (1582). Both mills are referred to as 'being of the said late Monastery of Wenlock'.
See Appendix 1, p. 69, entry for 1636 re Lacon family ownership of Aumers land.
**See reference to Masons Myll, Appendix 4, Item ii), Extract 1), p. 89.

The Farley millers referred to in the listing above could also have operated the watermill located at position 2 on the VCH seventeenth-century map on p. 82 (plot 268 of Foxall's map of 1847). The watermill, sited in the deep valley of Aclands Coppice, on a fast-flowing stream linked into Farley Brook in the vicinity of Lawley Cross, is likely to be the forge noted in the publication by Thomas Hearne[80] of John Leland's (1506–52) passage through Shropshire in the early sixteenth century:

> Yerne [iron] is made yn certen Places of Sbroffhirc (?) and especially yn the Wooddes betwixte Belvoys [Buildwas] and Wenloke [Wenlock]. Colys [coals] be diggid hard by Qmbridge^ where the Priory was.

K Jones[81] refers to a meeting on 2 March 1860, when a Mr Caleb Harper, the owner of Farley corn mill (position 1 on the VCH map), accepted the sum of £174 for his land in Farley. The land was required for construction of the proposed Wenlock and Severn Junction Railway line.

A 1933 edition of the Shrewsbury Chronicle also referred to a 'possible site [for the forge] in Farley Dingle, close to the railway, below the limeworks'.

The Bradley mill, recorded as a paper mill *c.*1770, would have been upstream of the forge and close to the parish/township boundary, indicated as location 3 on the VCH seventeenth-century map on p. 82. The remaining mill (position 1 on the VCH map) was likely to have been the mill located at the stream that runs alongside the existing road between Lawley Cross and Buildwas Abbey.

Before 1723 John Share (or Shore) appears to have held the lease on Bradley mill and 5 acres of land, along with use of Farley Common.

In 1723 Eldred L Lee is stated to be the holder of the lease, which ultimately passed to Sarah Windsor before 1774. Sarah Windsor (apparently) leased the paper mill, which was converted to an iron-mill (forge), to a man named Oram, a kinsman of Hallens of Harley Forge, and of Coalbrookdale and Hardwick Forge (S. Shrops.).

Richard Reynolds, a rich Quaker ironmaster with shares in the Ketley, Horsehay and Dale ironworks, is reputed to have taken over Oram's lease to ensure that it could not be open for lease to another as an ironworks.

Richard Reynolds of Coalbrookdale, possibly an earlier relative to Richard the father of Joseph and Hannah, built a forge on the site of a paper mill in *c.*1717.

In 1774 Sarah Windsor passed on the two remaining water mills to a William Jeffereys whose last will and testament (*c.* 30 Oct. 1783) reveals that '[he] gave and devised all those two water corn mills, called or known as Bradley mills, and a dwelling house and land in the parish of Much Wenlock, in the occasion of his son Edward Jeffereys, and which had been purchased from Mrs Sarah Windsor'.

These transactions appear to have coincided with the Darby family's ongoing developments in the method of iron production and ultimately the construction of the iron bridge in 1775–9.

A paper by Richard Hayman entitled 'The Shropshire Wrought-iron Industry *c.*1600–1900, A Study of Technology Change [p. 21] and [pp. 55-61] The Cranage Patent 1766' refers to the role of Richard Reynolds in the development of the iron industry at Coalbrookdale.

In 1824 Mrs Susan Jeffreys and son Richard sold the mills to Mr Thomas Harper. Thomas Harper & Son are recorded as 'working the mills' in 1851 but some years later the Harper family sold their mills and retired. Richard Jeffreys appears to have been 'a town or Wenlock miller' possibly at the Downs mill throughout the period 1817–50.

An entry in the Moseley Collection of Archives[82] reveals that 'William Childs, miller, of the [parish] of Buildwas' was 'the tenant of a property at Lawley Cross with a water corn mill and dressing mill near thereto, 3 pieces (5 acres) meadow and pasture at a rent of £26 5s yearly: £10 an acre newly ploughed'. The covenant notes that he had to leave the mills in 'good going' at the end of the lease of 19 years.

The succession of millers at the windmill between Richard Coundley (before 1685) and William Jeffreys, the miller prior to 1847 until its destruction in 1850, has yet to be identified. Jeffreys is noted as receiving eight years' compensation paid by Capt. Burlinson, the Wynnstay estate's land agent in 1858.

Accounts records[83] reveal that the Coal Brook Dale (Ironworks) was paid £1. 11s. 5d. for 'iron work for the Corn Mill', i.e. Downs Mill, as the windmill had ceased operation by 1850.

1321: Court-roll[84] of Wenlock Priory (in possession of Thomas Mytton, Esq. of Shipton) records:

> Magna Wenlock – Wednesday 28th Oct 1321, Robert de Bradenhop took a certain *place* of the Lord's *demesne,* described along with references to other localities e.g. Mardenole Street, Wyndmulnehull (Windmill Hill) and the Gardens of Vill, to hold for life at 10s. rent. Tenent to pay tithe and keep the land fenced. – *ingress-fee* 3s 4d. (The first known reference to a windmill on the site.)

1534: The Almoners Barn, a property on the Priory estate and a demesne mill, referred to as Mayres or Mayors (as mentioned in British History Online), were in the occupation of the Mayre family. In 1583 the mill comprised a pair of mills! This mill may have been sited in, or adjacent to, Almoners Croft (plot 161 of Foxall map, referred to on page 80) on a watercourse from the Pool Dam (Pouledame) as referred to in the Indenture document – Appendix 4 Historical Documents.

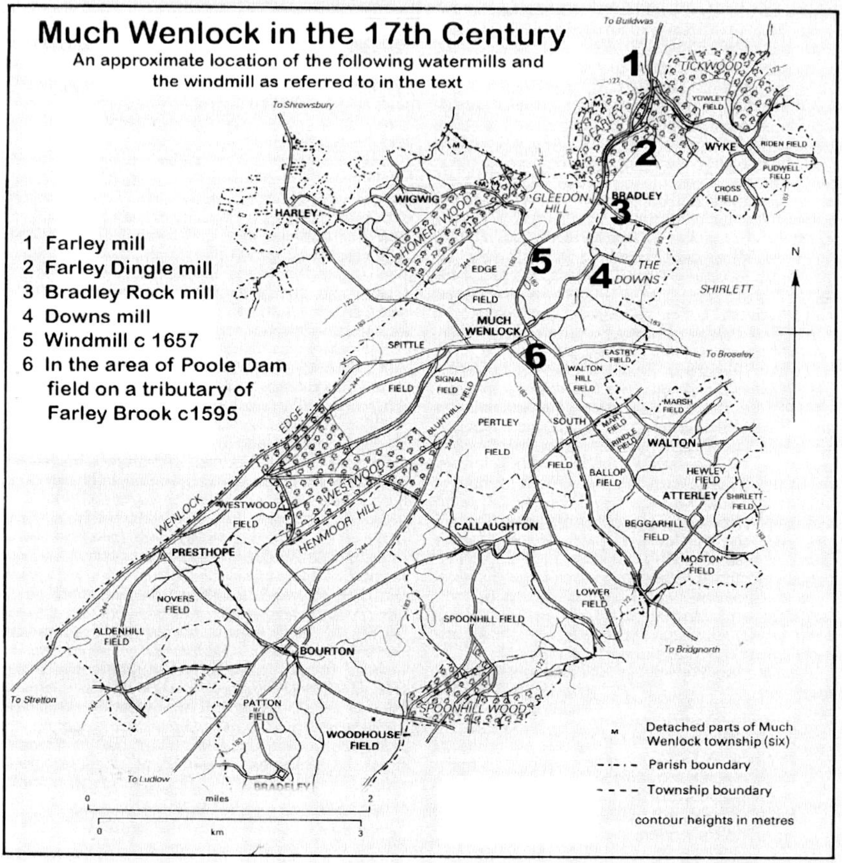

1536–7: According to VCH, Vol. X, pp. 431-2 the demesne mill stood on the Great Pool, retained by a dam on a tributary of Farley Brook.

1553: 'Mr Thomas Lawley stoped a corpse coming from Wyke at the brook at the grene myll coming the way through Barnesfold in a cart where the body remained til next day he was buryed'.[85]

This entry places the Grenemill with appurtenances at Downs Mill in the tenure of William Mare (see Appendix 4 Historical Documents).

1563: Wynnstay documents refer to a conveyance of a mill as Bridbacke – this may be Bradley Mill![86]

1564: The Greene Mill, a demesne mill, is referred to in the Elizabeth I grant document dated 1600. It has also been mentioned in the thirteenth century 'for serving the town'.

1600: The following extract is from a document,[87] granted and dated 23rd Feb. 42 Elizabeth I (see Appendix 4, Item i). p. 86).

> and whereas also in certain other our letters patent granted under our Great Seal of England bearing date at Westminster the first day of June in the thirty second year of our reign [1590] that we...express and specified delivered granted and to (farm) demised to Thomas Lawley, Edward Lawley and Anne Lawley. All that our mill called Greene Mill with the appurtenances situated And being in Wenlock...Formerly in the tenure or occupation of William More or his assigns And all that our watermill with appurtenances called Masons Mill situated and being in Wenlock aforesaid and the fishery to the same appertaining. And also all our lands meadows feedings pastures woods waters and commons tithes and hereditaments whatsoever to the same mill... Tenement and barn and our croft...Called Aumers Barnes in Wenlock in the late tenure of Thomas Mayre... which mills and other premises...etc... Are parcel of our Manor of Wenlock...To the said late Monastery... All houses edifices structures lofts crofts curtalages lands meadows feeding pastures commons waters water courses channels banks ponds fishponds fisheries fishings suit service and multure of tenants there profits commodities emoluments and hereditaments whatsoever to the said mills.
>
> Except however always and reserved to us our heirs and successors all great trees woods underwoods mines and quarries of the same premises... to the end and during the term of the life of him the said Thomas Lawley thereof after the decease... To the said Edward Lawley. Then to Anne Lawley. In witness whereof we have caused these our letters to be made patent witness ourselves at Westminster the twenty third day of February in the forty second year of our reign [1600].

1622–47: A windmill, possibly a malt mill, is referred to in NLW Wynnstay documents.[88]

1635: A paper mill stood beyond two pastures north-east of the Abbey, possibly in the Big Cow Meadow (Foxall, plot 165) and served by the pond within the meadow which ultimately fed into Farley Brook beyond the Fisheries. This is possibly the mill which Francis Selman occupied to make paper *c.*1702.

1639: A Mortgage by Release document[89] refers to a land transaction between Dame Ursula Bertie and Thomas Lawley of Twickenham which includes the 'Windmillhill Field', yet makes no reference to the stone tower windmill. This suggests the tower was a post-1639 construction.

Foxall's map of 1847 shows the 'Field adjoining Windmill Hill' as a separate parcel of land to Windmill Hill!

1647: An Estate Accounts document, Appendix 4, item iii), contains the reference 'Edward Embre the corne mill and the little meadow above yt. £17 10 0' and also refers to 'John Gower the lower orchard and the meadow towards the paper mill, £13 0 0'.

John Gower and Hugh Kinge also rented Poole Dam for £21.

This could place the paper mill at Poole Dam!

1661: John Clarke of Wyke, a paper maker, possibly at Bradley or at Farley mill.

1663: 'One milne called Enne Myll demised to William More. One water Mylne called Masons Mill with fishing to same with all pastures water and feedings etc. common to same with one barne and croft called Almers barne demised to Tho[mas] Mayre and Joanne his wife. One myll called Masons Myll in Bradley.
This sold by...Mary...To...?'[90]

The 'Indenture document', in Appendix 4 Historical Documents, item ii), includes the following note relating to corn mills:[91]

> the Upper part of Ruffe Downs then or late in the occupation of the said John Mason and the said mill called the Paper Mill and two other mills called the corn mill then or late in the occupation of the said John.

1670: A paper mill existed in close proximity to the Priory and was owned by John Mason.

1685: The will of the miller Richard Coundley the elder, who was renting the windmill from the estate owner Robert Bertie, bequests that 'all the right, tithe and interest I have in the windmill I now hold of my landlord Esquire Bertie unto my son, also named Richard, for the remainder of the lease'.

1709: 'Ann Hancock, mill for grinding bark' – the paper mill![92]

1714: The document 'Demesne Land of the Manor in Much Wenlock'[93] contains an entry:

> Richard Counley, 2 water grist mills and windmill, a dwelling house containing etc.

A further entry is as follows:

> Mr Richard Parsons, Isabel Smart widd. & John Roberts (rented) the Standhills wherein is the windmill and Bellow Leasow and Cutlers yard Meadow for £26 per annum.

Foxall's map of 1847 places the windmill at location 260 in Windmill Hill Field 259 with the Standhills at field locations 162 and 200-203, Bellow Leasow at 122-139 and Cutlers yard Meadow at 211.

Appendix 3 *History of Milling at Much Wenlock*

Mumford notes that the windmill stood one kilometre north of the town – this corresponds to location 260 (Foxall's map) and OS map SJ 629003.

1730: 'Joseph Hughes, late of Masons Mill'.[94]

1741: The windmill stood one km north of the town and appears on a map of the late Sir John Wynn's estate.[95]

1750: John Windsor was assigned Bradley farm including the mill – this was undoubtedly a watermill in ownership of the estate.

1774: Sarah Windsor, John's widow, assigned Birdbach (Bradley) mill to a William Jeffreys – this would be one of the estate's mills.

1815: The windmill was 'still working in 1815'.[96]

1847: The Foxall Tithe Apportionment indicates that Sir Watkin Williams Wynn owned the Windmill Hill land and it was occupied by Benjamin Ainsworth. Sir Watkin also owned Downs Mill farmland which was occupied by William Jeffreys.

1850: William Jeffreys rented the mill (the windmill?) and the water-mill at Downs farm, '...The windmill was, apparently, wrecked by lightning *c.*1850.'

This may have been the malt mill mentioned 1622–47.[97]

1858: A Wynnstay document[98] listing payments in Wenlock reveals that Wm. Jeffreys was paid compensation for the loss of the windmill which was struck by lightning, the payment being made by Captain Burlinson, land agent for the Wynnstay estate, 'Being 8 years at £5 and a total of £40'.

Appendix 4

Historical Documents

i) Extracts of Grant from Queen Elizabeth to Thomas and Robert Lawley of the Manor of Wenlock. 23rd Feby. 42 Elizabeth[99]
ii) Extracts from an Indenture made thirteenth day of June in the Fifteenth year of the Reign of Charles the Second.[100]
iii) Extracts of Estate Accounts of Wenlock in 1647[101]
iv) Extracts from the full transcript of Will and Testament of Robert Bertie 1695[102]
v) Extracts from a Survey of the Manor *circa* 1700[103]

i) Extracts of Grant from Queen Elizabeth to Thomas and Robert Lawley of the Manor of Wenlock 23rd Feby 42 Elizabeth (1600)

The following selected extracts provide an insight into the Lawley family involvement in land and property management in Much Wenlock during the late sixteenth to mid seventeenth centuries.

Extract (p. 1) Elizabeth by the Grace of God of England France and Ireland Queen Defender of the Faith. TO ALL to whom these present letters shall come, Greeting.

WHEREAS in certain our letters patent granted under our Great Seal of England bearing date Gorhamburye the twelfth day of July in the eleventh year of our Reign (1569) it is mentioned that we by our same letters patent for the consideration in the same letters patent expressed and specified delivered granted and the farm demised to William Doddington Gentleman.

[Various messuages and tenements with the appurtenances, land, crofts and pastures along with recipients are identified. All properties and land are stated as being in Wenlock and [part of the late Priory of Wenlock]]

Extract (p. 2) AND WHEREAS ALSO in certain other our letters patent granted under our Great Seal of England bearing date at Westminster the twenty sixth day of February in the twenty fourth year of our Reign (26th Feb 1582) it is mentioned that we by the same letters patent bearing date the same twenty sixth day of February in the aforesaid twenty fourth year of our Reign for the consideration in the same letters patent expressed and specified delivered and granted and to farm demised To Thomas Lawley amongst other things all that rent of assize or chief rent going out of the lands and tenements of a certain Thomas Smith in Great Wenlock in the county of Salop And all those our messuages lands and tenements in Wenlock aforesaid then or late in the tenure or occupation of diverse persons [*as identified in the transcript of original document*] there demised by Copy of Court according to the custom of the Manor there And also those lands and tenements in Wenlock aforesaid,

In the several tenures or occupations of diverse persons there at will And also all that our messuages or tenements called Hillhouse with the appurtenance situate lying and being in the town and fields of Great Wenlock aforesaid And one cottage and a little croft to the same appertaining with appurtenances then or late in the tenure or occupation of Thomas Byll or his assigns.

Extract (p. 3) And also certain our lands and pastures there called Aumers ground...in the tenure of Thomas Haywarde alias Heywarde...And all that our tenement...in Winmerestreete alias Burland late in the tenure...of Margaret Locker...Also a tenement there called Digginhall and all lands to the same in tenure of Richard Nedle and Catherine his wife...And all that our mill called Grenemill with the appurtenances – tenure of William Mare – And all that our water mill called Masons Myll and the fisheries there and all our lands meadows feedings and pastures woods waters and commons And all our barn and croft called Aumers Barn – tenure or occupation of Thomas Manne alias Mayer Joan his wife and Thomas and Catherine their children And also all those lands and tenements there with the appurtenances of which the rents were late paid to the Office of Chamberlain of the late Monastery of Wenlock aforesaid.

Extract (p. 4) TO HAVE and to hold the aforesaid rent messuages tenements lands meadows feedings pastures services stables closes and all and singular other the premises with all their appurtenances except as by the same letters patent before excepted to the aforesaid Thomas Lawley...until the end and during the term of twenty one years...RENDERING annually to us our heirs and successors...Twenty six pounds eleven shillings and ten pence for the services of our Chaplain in the parish church of Great Wenlock...

Extract (p. 5) To have and to hold the aforesaid mills and other the premises... during the term of the life of him the said Thomas Lawley and his assigns from the making of the same our letters patent to the end and during the term of the life of him the said Thomas remainder thereof after the deceased surrender or forfeiture of the said Thomas Lawley to the aforesaid Edward Lawley and his assigns to the end and during the term of life of her the said Anne RENDERING YEARLY to us our heirs and successors of and for the aforesaid mill called Grene Myll with the appurtenances twenty three shillings And of and for the aforesaid Mill called Masons Myll and other the premises...the aforesaid barn and croft called Aumers Barne with the appurtenances thirty six shillings and nine pence of lawful money of England at the feast of Saint Michael...Paid by equal portions during the term aforesaid...And after the decease of any of the aforesaid Thomas

Edward and Anne...THEN RENDERING to us our heirs and successors the best Beast of the person who shall so depart this life in the name of a heriot...

Extract (p. 7) KNOW YE that we for and in consideration of the sum of one thousand three hundred and twenty pounds fifteen shillings and eight pence of lawful money of England at the receipt of our Exchequer into the hands of our well beloved servant Edward Carey Knight one of the tellers of our same Exchequer to our use by our well beloved subjects Thomas Lawley Esquire and Robert Lawley Gentleman in hand well and faithfully paid whereof we acknowledge ourselves to be fully satisfied and paid And the same Thomas Lawley and Robert Lawley their executors and administrators therefrom to be forever acquitted and exonerated by these presents of our special grace and certain knowledge and mere motion...

Extract (p. 11) We further give and by these presents for us our heirs and successors do grant to the aforesaid Thomas Lawley and Robert Lawley their heirs and assigns the aforesaid Manor chantry mills messuages tenements and all and singular other the premises hereinbefore by these presents granted with all their appurtenances as fully freely and entirely and in as ample manner and form as all and singular the premises or any parcel thereof to our hands or to the hands of our very dear father and brother Henry the Eighth and Edward the Sixth late Kings of England or to the hands of either of them or to the hands of our very dear sister Mary late Queen of England by reason or on account of the dissolution or surrender of any late Monasteries or Priories or by reasons or on account of any pre-requisition or of any gift or grant or of any attainder or forfeiture or by reason or on account of any Act of Parliament. ...EXCEPT...All that tenement with one close and fifty acres of land situated and lying and being in Great Wenlock appertaining or belonging late in the tenure of one Richard Dawley or his assigns.

*ii) Extracts from an Indenture made thirteenth day of June in the Fifteenth year of the Reign of Charles the Second.**

{BRACKETS} reflect doubtful or not yet decipherable script.
Italics denote names of land parcels.
Entries in **bold type** identify relevant names and parcels of land.
NB All spellings are translated to modern style.
Bracketed [names or numeric dates] added by the author.

Extract 1) This Indenture made the thirteenth day of June in the fifteenth year of the Reign of our sovereign Lord Charles the Second in the year of lord of England Scotland France and Ireland king defender of the faith and realm And in the year of our Lord one thousand and six hundred threescore and three [1663] BETWEEN Sir Cyril Wyche of London knight one of the six {clerks} of his majesty's High Court of Chancery Sir Henry Oxinden of Deane in the parish of Wingham in the

---

*During the reign of Charles II all legal documents, including this one, were dated as if his reign had begun from his father's (Charles I) date of execution in 1649 (Ref:Wikipedia.org/wiki/charles_II_of_England).

county of Kent knight **Squire George Penruddock** of Broad Chalke in the county of Wilts. Knight and **the honourable Dame Ursula** his wife of the one part And the honourable Frances Belasyse sister of the right honourable Thomas lord 2nd Viscount Earl Fauconberg of the other part WHEREAS the said Sir George Penruddock by the name of **George Penruddock** of Broad Chalke in the county of Wilts. Esquire and the said Dame Ursula by the name of **Dame Ursula Bertie** his wife Robert Laworth of Gray's Inn in the county of Middlesex Sir Martin Noell of London knight by the name of Martin Noell and William Seaman of London Merchants by their Indenture bearing date the nine and twentieth day of May in the year of our lord one thousand six hundred fifty and three [1653] for the consideration therein mentioned DID bargain and sell unto the said Sir Henry Oxinden by the name of Henry Oxinden Esquire son heir apparent of Sir James Oxinden of Deane in the parish of Wingham in the county of Kent knight and the said Sir Cyril Wyche by the name of Cyril Wyche of London gent ALL that the gift of the late priory of Great Wenlock with the appurtenance in the county of Salop and all messuages dove house and other houses barns stables and offices buildings gardens and yards orchards backside lands tenements and hereditament within the said site of the said late priory or to the same at any time belonging or appertaining or to or with the...{usually}...demised or seffen or accepted reputed or taken as part parcel or member thereof or of any part thereof And all those messuages cottages closes meadows pastures land tenements and hereditament within their and every of their appurtenance within the town or parish of Much Wenlock in the said county of Salop hereafter mentioned that is to say All those two pastures lying northeastward between the capital messuage usually called the **priory house and a certain mill called the paper mill [Masons Myll ?]** then or late in the occupation of **{Elleanor Kinaston}** widow And all that cottage or tenement wherein one **William Dawley yeoman** then or late did inhabit And all that meadow usually called or known by the name of ***Pouldame*** And all...

Extract 2) that part of pasture ground called or known by the name of ***Cutlers yard*** and two acres of arable and pasture ground usually called or known by the name of the ***Two Sandhills*** and the conyney thereupon and part of a meadow called the ***Broad Meadow*** And two other meadows the one called the ***Bellhole*** and the other the ***Mills meadow...***

Extract 3) And one pasture ground usually called or known by the name of ***Lercroft*** then or late in the occupation of **George Adney vicar** And one pasture ground called ***The Further Downs*** then or late in the tenure or occupation of **John Mason** And one pasture ground usually called or known by the name the ***Upper part of Ruffe Downs*** then or late in the occupation of the said **John Mason** And the said **Mill called the Paper Mill and two other mills called the Corn Mills then or late in the occupation of the said John Mason...**

Extract 4) and all that arable land called ***Walton Hill Pasture*** and ***Ruffe Downs*** then or late in the occupation of the said **Sir George Penruddock** and **Dame Ursula** his wife or one of their heirs or one of their assigned And all that pasture ground usually called or known by the name of ***The Avenors Croft*** then or late in the occupation of the said **Sir George Penruddock** and **Dame Ursula** his wife their or one of their assigned...

Extract 5) And all that land and tenements confining by **Shienton** one hundred and two acres more or less usually called or known by the name or names lying within the fields or furlongs of ***Windmill Smithfield Edgefield*** and ***Shinewhead*** furlong or any of them And all that land and tenements confining by one hundred four and twenty acres more or less usually called or known by the name or names lying within the fields or furlongs usually called or known by the name or names of ***Bradley Furlong*** and ***Knightstreetfield...***

Extract 6) And all other messuages lands tenements and hereditament in the premise Indenture of sale bearing the sixteenth day of March in the tenth year [1659] of the reign of the late King Charles were demised or intended to be demised by the said Dame Ursula to one **{Ralph} Bradley** And the reversion and reversioned remainder and un-remained yearly and other rents and profits {referred} due and payable upon any demised or remaining lease or leased of the site or any part or parcel thereof TO HAVE AND TO HOLD all and singular the said site messuages lands and premise and every part and parcel thereof thereby mentioned and intended to be thereby bargained and sold with their and every of their appurtences unto the said Sir Henry Oxinden and Sir Cyril Wyche their executors administrators and assigned from henceforth during the term of one thousand years next ensuing and fully to be completed and ended without of or for any manner of wast...

Extract 7) AND IT IS to be wanted concluded and agreed by and between all and every the said { } to these present that the said Sir George Penruddock and Dame Ursula his wife their heirs and assigned shall and may hold and enjoy the said site messuages lands and premises and receive and take the rents {issues} and profits thereof to their or one of their own use and used until default shall be made in payment of the said {feudal} sums of threescore pounds and two thousand and threescore pounds or one of them or form part of them or one of them contrary to the promise covenant and agreement aforesaid and the true intent and meaning of these presents without the lawful sell suite trouble molestation interruption or disturbance of the said Frances Belasyse her executors and administrators and or assigned or any other persons lawfully claiming or to claim by from or under her them or any of them in witness whereof the parties first above named to these presence indenture interchangeably their hand & seals have set the day & year first above written.

Sealed and delivered by the within named
Sir Geo. Penruddock & Dame Ursula his wife in the presence of (3 signatures)
Sir Henry Oxinden in the presence of (5 signatures)
Cyril Wyche in the presence of (4 signatures)

(NB The original document contains all of the signatures)

Appendix 4 *Historical Documents*

iii) Extracts of Estate Accounts of Wenlock in 1647

(A handwritten note on page 1 of the document is as follows with modern spelling inserted)

> Madam this paper is a note delivered by my wife's servants as they did let the several parcels the last year I can assure your Ladyship it is all in the mortgage and more. I am troubled I can at present give your Ladyship no better satisfaction my wife having disposed herself of her writings [words crossed out] and the recorder who hath them being now out of the town but if anything be required of me I am most ready to perform it and remain madam
>
> Your Ladyships most humble servant
>
> [signed] Geo. Penruddocke

NB An interpretation of the above document would be that Penruddocke's first wife may have performed an administrative role for Dame Bertie's property portfolio. All of her papers were with the recorder so Penruddocke provided information from papers to hand covering tenancy and land rental charges.

A further note states:

> Memorand that we Richard Field, Gent. James Lewes Christopher Morrall by authority from George Penruddock Esq. have set the Honourable Lady Berties demesne land at Wenlock to the several tenants hereafter for the several rents at their several names appearing for one whole year from and after the 25th day of March next 1647.

Amongst the listed entries are:

Edward Embree the corne mill and the little meadow above yt £17 10s. 0d.
John Gower the Lower Orchard and the meadow towards the paper mill £13 0s. 0d.
John Gower and Hugh Kinge the Poole Dam £21 0s. 0d.

There is unset the Almoners Croft and the Middle Meadow, used to be set to him that holds the Malt Mill.
Joyce Watkin pays for one quarter £4 15s and Ed. Emory and Jos. Cooke pays the other three quarters [sent to Sir Edward Lawley] £21 10s. 0d

iv) *An extant copy of the original will of Robert Bertie, Esq. {bearing} Mr Gage by Title to the Manor of Wenlock 14th Dec. 1699. Will prepared 23rd Dec. 1695, the original remaining in the Prerogative Office 10th March 1713*

NB Words in brackets { }indicate an unsure transcription; empty brackets as ( ) indicate no transcription and]1 indicates the end of copy document page.

The following abbreviated extracts reflect the main beneficiaries to the will.

Extract (p. 1)
Robert Bertie lately of the Middle Temple London committing the (necessary) preamble of a Will I do make this my last Will and Testament in manner and form following imprimis I give devise and bequeath unto my nephew Thomas Gage and the heirs of his body begotten All that my Manor of Great Wenlock in the County of Salop with all its rights appurtenants and appurtenances whatsoever hereunto belonging or any wise appertaining as also all my lands tenements and hereditament mills messuages houses and crofts in Great]1Wenlock and Bradley and the parishes adjacent thereunto in the said County of Salop with the Court Leet and Court Baron of and in Great Wenlock with all Rights Royalties Privileges conney of all sorts and kinds fishings watercourses emoluments profits interests either in law or equity whatsoever whether in possession reversion or remainder belonging any wise or appertaining unto the said manor lands tenements and hereditaments aforesaid or commonly used herewith as also my Rectory or Parsonage impropriate of Great Wenlock aforesaid and the presentee to the vicarage of]2 Wenlock aforesaid and also tithes of all sorts and kinds whatsoever as likewise my farms of Blakeway and {Prees} in the said County of Salop...

Extract (p. 4)
in the said County of Salop in what parish or parishes (...) or (...) whatsoever or whosoever they be to have and to hold all the said (...) together with all and every their appurtenants and appurtenances unto the said Thomas Gage and the heirs of his body begotten and for want of such issue I devise and bequeath to my nephew Joseph Edward Gage and the heirs of his body begotten the said manor farms lands]4 tenements and hereditaments copy holds rectory and parsonage impropriate of Wenlock aforesaid presentee to the said vicarage of Wenlock.

Extract (p. 5)
aforesaid and of all and every other the premises above specified in as large and ample manner and form to all intents (...) and purposes as I have before and above expressed to my said nephew Thomas Gage To have and to hold the said premises with all and every their appurtenants and appurtenances unto the said Joseph Edward Gage and the heirs of his body begotten and for want of such]5 issue I devise and bequeathed unto my nephew John Gage and the heirs of his body...begotten the said manor farms lands tenements and hereditaments

copy holds rectory or parsonage impropriate of Wenlock aforesaid presentee to the said vicarage of Wenlock aforesaid and all and every other the premises above specified in as large and ample manner and form to all intent (...) and purposes as I have before and above expressed to my said nephew Thomas Gage To have and to hold the said premises with all and every]6 their appurtenants and appurtenances unto the said John Gage and the heirs of his body begotten and for want of such issue...

Extract (p. 7)
I devise and bequeath unto my niece Elizabeth Gage and the heirs of her body...

Extract (p. 8)
I devise and bequeath unto my niece Ann Gage and the heirs of her body...

Extract (p. 13)
I give to my nephew John Gage...and my brother Edward Penruddocks...my cousin Mrs Sussanna {Barnell}...my cousin Perigrine Bertie...my Uncle Robert Bertie and to Uncle Montague lately Chief Baron and to my cousin Charles Bertie...and to my sister-in-law Mrs Joan {Vance} and to my kinsman Sir Francis Lawley and to my old friend Mr Humphrey {Michell} of Richmond in Surrey and to Mr William Longville a Bencher of the Inner Temple mourning rings to each and every of those severally to be provided]14 by my Executor and to be of the weight of thirty shillings in gold apiece besides the (...) to Mr William {Thursby} a Bencher of the Middle Temple I give all the Law books I lent him comprised in a catalogue I believe left in his hands to Mr John Carson Vicar of Great Wenlock in the County of Salop...to Mr John Mason my present Bailiff in Wenlock if he maintains my Bailiff at the time of my demise I give...to my servant]15 John Smith if he lives with me at the time of my demise I give...To Mrs Carter that lived in the Abbey I give...To the Widow Wilroy that lives in the Abbey I give... the parish of Great Wenlock aforesaid I give twenty pounds to be disposed of by the Vicar of Wenlock aforesaid...

I give and bequeath all the rest and residue of my goods and chattels money arrearages of Rent Debts and personal estate whatsoever not before disposed of]17 my former legatees and bequests being first discharged and paid unto my said nephew Joseph Edward Gage his Executors Administrators and Assigns I desire to be buried in the Chancel of the parish church of Great Wenlock aforesaid in some dry place thereof and to have a flat tombstone of marble laid over me with an inscription signifying that I be buried in that place lastly I do constitute and appoint my brother-in-law Joseph Gage that married my sister the sole Executor of this my last Will and Testament]18 and do hereby give unto my said brother three hundred pounds of good money desiring and requesting him to manage with all care and to the best advantage and profit my real and personal estate before given by and unto his children until they attain the age of twenty one years or marriage before the said age and for his so doing to reimburse himself of all costs and charges that he shall expend thereabout and their several and respective estates {legatees} and bequests before severally given unto them in witness hereof]19 I have herewith set my hand and sole this three and twentieth day of December in the year of our lord one thousand six hundred and ninety and five [23 Dec. 1695] ROBERT BERTIE signed sealed and published by the within

named Robert Bertie in our presence and attested and subscribed by us in the presence of the said Robert Bertie the day and year above mentioned
Henry North, Walter Booden, {Sir} {Rigmaiden}, John Smith

A footnote, in Latin, is added here dated 1698.

A further note was included as follows:
This is a copy of the Will of Robert Bertie Esq. Extant and agreeing with the original Will remaining in the Prerogative office the 10th day of March 1713 by me {signed James Evans}

v) Extracts from a Survey of the Manor of Much Wenlock in the County of Salop, prepared by John Reynolds

The date of 1717 included on p. 11 of the survey document presumably denotes the date at which the document was compiled reflecting tenancies from 1600 to 1695.

The survey records provide a detailed insight to the local socio-economic environment of the seventeenth century and the interrelationship between landlords and tenants, also between tenants where subletting is involved. The complete document provides an insight into copyhold in English law[104] in relation to tenancy arrangements.

Records show that there were 51 tenants having a cottage in the manor. Details of the leases and location of the properties are included in the document (pp. 1-17 inclusive).

A detailed description of the property, the associated land where applicable, and whether it was arable, meadow or pasture land, is also registered. The acreage involved is given along with the annual rental charge. The survey document includes a comprehensive description of the manor house and its associated outbuildings.

Land usage within a 'reputed area' comprised 6 acres, at an annual rent of £10. A dwelling house, associated outbuildings, and land area including a reference to the windmill rented by Richard Counley or Coundley are included. The rent is shown as £27.

A copy of the original will and testament of Richard Counley, miller, dated 1685, refers to his mills:

> I assign and set over all the right, title and interest I have in the mills I now hold of my landlord Esquire Bertie, and the same to have and to hold the said mills, 2 water grist mills and windmill, unto my son Richard for and during the remainder of years yet to come.

The Manor Survey document (pp. 18-36) provides details of 'Reversions of Much Wenlock after Single Lives', naming the lives and description of their lands and tenements. References are made to various tradespeople, the town clerk and the vicars.

The town clerk, a Mr Thomas Smith, is shown to have occupied:

> Bru{ry} Leasow, 7 acres of pasture land @ £4. 17s. 6d.
> the meadow next Blakes meadow comprising 5 acres of meadow land @ £6. 10s. 0d.
> the Little meadow comprising 2 acres of meadow land @ £2. 10s. 0d.

The following vicars and their patrons are:

> Thomas Lawley, Gent, Patron to George Adeney as vicar of Wenlock in 1616.
> Lady Ursula Bertie (née Lawley) Patron to Josiah Bell, the vicar of Wenlock in 1664.
> Robert Bertie, arm, Patron to John Parsons in 1682.

Mr Thomas Baker, BA, whose patron is noted as the Bishop, was vicar of the town in 1706 and recorded as holding the tenancy of the New Tinings, comprising 5 acres of pasture land @ £1. 15s. 0d.

A further record relating to the vicar is:

> Vicar for the schoolhouse built at his charge, Mrs Spratts, and other charitable persons for teaching the children, @ 2s. 0d.

A typical sample entry reveals that, on 6 Oct. 1602, Robert Bertie granted a lease to John Parsons, clerk, who appears to have sublet to Mrs Ann Bell, a spinster aged 40, a messuage containing:

> 2 ground floor rooms, 1 brewhouse, 1 shop, 2 butterys, 4 chambers, a work-house for a skinner and a room over it, 1 backside, 1 garden and various parcels of land [named] which include spittlefield.

A further entry relates to Mr Richard Parsons, Isobel Smart widow and John Roberts 'for the Standhills, wherein is the windmill and Bellow Leasow and Cutlers Yard'. The rental for the 7 acres (2.84 ha) of meadow land is stated as £26.The Windmill Hill site is immediately adjacent to the area known as the Standhills.

The Manor Survey document (pp. 18-36 inclusive) covers the 'Reversions of Much Wenlock after Single Lives', detailing names of the lives and description of their lands and tenements. Also included are references to whom {the Lord} leased the property – buildings and land – and to whom it was subleased (if appropriate). The date of the lease is included and in some instances an indication of whether the reversion was for a single life or three lives or the remainder of a 99-year lease. The following notes summarise the Bertie and the Penruddocke /Bertie family involvement in property-leasing 1600–1700.

Two samples of lease arrangements are presented below for comparison purposes, one for the year 1600 and one in the year 1695 [£ included for clarity].

1600: 24 Aug – Robert Bertie, 1st Earl of Lindsey (b. 1583, d. 1642) *(first recorded lease by Robert Bertie)* William Bryan, aged 50, Tobacco pipe maker – Bryant's Tenements

A sample entry in the manor survey document reads:

> William Bryan & Joyce Taylor of Acton Round holds a messuage and tenement of (4) ground rooms, 3 chambers, 1 stable and 1 backside.
> *Chief Rents or*
> *Rents Reserved*: £2. 0s. 0d. or 1(one) hen at Shrovetide or 2s. 0d. at the lord's election.
> *Herriots:* 10s. 0d. on the death or alienation or discharge of every principal tenant.
> *Improved rent or value beyond same:* £2. 0s. 0d.

An abbreviated list of entries continues:

1600: 17 Sept – Robert Bertie to Joseph Bruce
1602: 2 Oct – Robert Bertie to Thomas Harryman, dec'd & Mary Harryman
1602: 16 Oct – Robert Bertie to John Parsons, clerk, dec'd
1602: 20 Oct – Robert Bertie to John Andrews, dec'd
1602: 20 Oct – Robert Bertie to Edward Wilkinson
1602: 20 Oct – Robert Bertie to Samual Jones, dec'd
1603: 20 Aug – Robert Bertie to Josiah Morrall, dec'd & John Parson, clerk, dec'd
1603: 13 Sept – Robert Bertie to Richard Bagshaw
1604: ? ? – Robert Bertie to John Parsons, dec'd
1604: 20 Sept – Robert Bertie to Thomas Bowdler
1604: 20 Sept – Robert Bertie to Henry Blake, dec'd
1604: 20 Sept – Robert Bertie to Lewis Davis, vicar, the Wood House
1604: 20 Dec – Robert Bertie to Edward (?), dec'd
1605 Robert Bertie, 1st Earl of Lindsey married Elizabeth Montague (d. 1654)
Circa 1605 Sir Edward Lawley married Susan Fisher
1606: 20 Sept – Robert Bertie granted lease to William Parsons
Circa 1606 Ursula Lawley, daughter of Sir Edward & Susan, born
1608 Montagu Bertie, 2nd Earl of Lindsey, son of Robert, d. 1666
1609: 20 Aug – Robert Bertie to J. Morrall (dec'd) and John Parsons, dec'd
1622: 16 Sept – Robert Bertie to Thomas Reynolds (or 1672?)
1625 Ursula Lawley married Sir Roger Bertie, KB
1626 Robert Bertie, son of Ursula & Sir Roger, born
1636: 10 April – Dame Ursula Bertie to John Hughes
1st recorded lease by Dame Ursula Bertie
1642 Ursula's husband, Robert Bertie, 1st Earl of Lindsey, died
1646 Ursula's second marriage to Sir George Penruddocke
1649: 20 Oct – Geo. Penruddocke & Dame Ursula to Jasper Clovely, dec'd
1st recorded joint lease of G Penruddocke & Dame Ursula
1649: 20 Oct – Geo. Penruddocke & Dame Ursula Bertie to Edward Andrews,

cornwagoner, dec'd
1649: 10 Nov – Geo. Penruddocke & Dame Ursula Bertie to John Gower
1654 Sir Roger Bertie died 15. 10. 54; will dated 8 July 1654
Elizabeth Bertie née Montague died 30. 11. 54
1657: 20 Mar – Geo. Penruddocke & Dame Ursula Bertie to Aaron Meredith
1657: 14 Apr – Geo. Penruddocke & Dame Ursula Bertie to Edward Thompson Butcher, dec'd
1657: 2 May – Geo. Penruddocke & Ursula Bertie to Hugh King, father of Isabel Sherrington
1657: 4 May – Geo. Penruddocke & Dame Ursula, his wife, to Thomas Barber and widow Barber
1657: 10 May – Geo. Penruddocke to Robert Powell & John Holder of London
1657: ? Aug – Geo. Penruddocke & Dame Ursula to Richard Bird, dec'd
1660: 1 Mar – Dame Ursula Bertie to Humphrey Clevelly, Walter Dakin & George Carver
1660: 1 Sept – Geo. Penruddocke & Dame Ursula Bertie to Francis Haywood, dec'd
1661: 29 Sept – Geo. Penruddocke & Dame Ursula Bertie to Humphrey Palmer, last recorded lease by both parties, dec'd
Bargain & Sell signed between Sir Cyril Wyche, Sir Henry Oxinden & Sir George Penruddocke and Dame Ursula his wife on one part and the Honourable Francis Belasyse, sister of Thomas Belasyse, 2nd Viscount Fauconberg.
1664 Sir George Penruddocke died
1665: 24 June – Dame Ursula Bertie to Thomas Sutton of London, victualler
1667: 24 May – Blakeway farm at Blakeway in the parish of Harley in the county of Salop in the tenure of Richard Lee as tenant at will from Lady Day to Lady Day. The farm was let by lease dated 24 May 1667 by Dame Ursula Bertie to Richard Lee, the sitting tenant's grandfather, for 99 years or 3 lives or either of them should so long live
1669: 15 July – Dame Ursula Bertie to Sam Enchmond
1669: 19 July – Dame Ursula Bertie to Sarah Archibold, widow dec'd
1669: ? ? – Dame Ursula Bertie to Ann Mason (aged 70 yrs) widow, now Ann Sproat widow & son Joseph Mason (50 yrs) ironmonger, holds a messuage in Wilmore Street containing 5 ground rooms, 4 chambers, 1 meadow of 3 rood, at Barrow Street end at an 'Improved rent or value beyond the same' of £4. 0s. 0d.
1670: 1 July – Dame Ursula Bertie to Richard Morrall
1671: 1 June – Dame Ursula Bertie to Thomas Bowdler, senior
1672: 2 ? – Dame Ursula Bertie to John Rubry, cornwagoner
1672: 10 June – Dame Ursula Bertie to Margaret King, widow dec'd
1676: 15 Dec – Dame Ursula Bertie to Francis Morrall Tanner
1676: 26 Dec – Dame Ursula Bertie to Francis Morrall, dec'd
1677: 15 May – Dame Ursula Bertie to Isabel Taylor
1679: 10 June – Dame Ursula to Ralph Wood
1685 see above p. 000 for Richard Counley & Mr Richard Parsons, etc. leases
1685 Dame Ursula died
1686: 1 Sept – Robert Bertie to John Day
1690: 20 Mar – Robert Bertie to John Phillips
1695: 20 Mar – Robert Bertie to John Mason (aged 50) and his son Thomas (21 yrs) – The Hill Tenement. The extent of the tenancy being a messuage of

4 ground rooms, 1 cellar, 4 chambers at a rent of £5. 0s. 0d. and 1 garden, orchard & pound yard, parts of a (?) thereunto adjoining at a rent of £1. 0s. 0d.

John Mason appears to have sublet property and land to Edward Southerne; Rowland Willnor*; John Jones; James Chaddock and George {Ropier}.

The detail of each of the four sublets, included in the document, reveals the total of the widely dispersed land parcels amounts to: 48 acres of arable land, 5 acres and 1 rood meadow land 27 acres and 9 roods of pasture land.

1699 Robert Bertie, son of Dame Ursula, died (dsp)

1717: The Manor Survey document records John Mason as a tenant at will in Spittle Street with the property comprising:

A messuage consisting 2 ground rooms & buttery, 2 chambers, 1 barne & stable, 4 bay, 1 garden & home close. Let to Geo. Smith at £2. 10s. 0d. John Mason's additional holdings at the date of the Survey included:

The Stockings at Westwood gate, 9 rood pasture land at £4. 10s. 0d.
The other Stockings & little close under (   ) at £1. 0s. 0d.
Halfe the barn and 1 bay at £6. 5s. 0d.
(L)odge croft and 4 acres and 2 rood of arable land at £1. 3s. 0d.
In the Southfields, 1 acre and 2 rood of arable land.
In Pearly fields, 3 acres and 2 rood at 11s. 0d.
In Knightstree fields, 2 acres of arable land at 6s. 0d.
In Spittlefields under (   ) arable, 4 acres at 12s. 0d.
Lodge Croft close, 1 acre and 1 rood of meadow land at £1. 0s. 0d.
A Close at Blakeway Lane head, 1 acre and 2 rood at £1. 0s. 0d.
In Spittle Fields now 3 houses built thereon, 1 acre of pasture In the possession of Dorothy Smith widdow at 2s. 0d. and Widdow Jones at 2s. 0d., Abraham Jones 2s. 0d.
John Simons a house at Penny Croft at 3s. 4d.
Adam James at Farley Head in Common fields at £1. 0s. 0d.
George Morrall the Knowle inclosed at Westwood, 9 acres pasture, 2 Great Butts in Spittle Fields and 2 gully in Edgefield 3 rood of arable land at 12s. 0d.

*Rowland Willnor's cottage [and additional facilities] attracted:

Chief Rents or
Rents Reserved: £5. 0s. 0d. couple of capons, couple of hens at Shrovetide or 3s. 6d. at the lord's election.

Herriots: Best cow or £2. 10s. 0d. at the lord's election on death or alienation or exchange.

Improved rent or value beyond same: covering the total of John Mason's initial lease £31. 1s. 0d.

References

Introduction

1 Langdon, J., *Mills in the Medieval Economy: England 1300–1540* (Oxford, OUP, 2004).

Chapter 2

2 Gregory, T., *The Shropshire Gazetteer: A Survey of the County & Valuable Miscellaneous Information* (Gregory, Wem, 1824), with plates, pp. 342-5.

3 Anderson, J. C., *Shropshire, its early history and antiquities* (London, Willis & Southeran, 1864), p. 239

4 Randall, J., *Randall's Tourist's Guide to Wenlock* with photographic & wood illustrations (Madeley, Randall, 1875), p. 52; pp. 5-54; pp. 137-40.

5 Lloyd, L. C., *Borough of Wenlock 1468–1968* (1968).

6 Money, J., 'Taverns, Coffee Houses and Clubs; Local politics and popular Articulacy in the Birmingham Area in the Age of the American Revolution' (*The Historical Journal*, 14, II, 1971, pp. 15-47).

7 http://www.tudorplace.com.ar/BERTIE.htm

8 Bertie Family Papers in Ancaster Deposits documents, p. 13. Historical Manuscript Commission (HMC), Anc. pp. 476 -7; Anc. 7a/8c and e.

9 Nichol, J. D., 'Wynnstay, Willey and Wenlock: A Study in Local Political History' (*Shropshire Archaeological and Historical Society*, 58, 1965–8, pp. 220–27).

10 British History Online: Victoria County History, 'The Liberty and Borough of Wenlock: The Borough 1468–1836 ' (VCH Shropshire, 10, 1998, ed. C. R. J. Currie, pp. 187-212).

11 Foxall, H. D. G., '1847 Tithes Apportionment Map of Wenlock Township'.

12 Bryer, R. A., 'Roots of Modern Capitalism: A Marxist Accounting History of the origins and consequences of Capitalist Landlords in England' (*The Accounting Historians Journal*, June 2004). Paper available online 26 January 2005.

13 Donnachie, I. L., and Stewart, Norma K., 'Scottish Windmills – An outline & inventory' (*Scottish Committee on Industrial Archaelogy*, 1964, p. 285).

14 Gaskell, Lady C. Milnes, *Spring in a Shropshire Abbey* (London, Smith, Elder, 1905), p. 69.

15 Beckett, J. V., 'Aristocrats & Electoral Control in the East Midlands 1660–1914' (*University of Nottingham*).

16 'A Green and Pleasant Land' (*History of British Landscapes and Countryside*, Part 4) www.countrylovers.co.uk/places/histland4.htm

Chapter 3

17 Eyton, R. W., *Antiquities of Shropshire* (London, J. R. Smith,1854).

18 Cox, D. C., 'The Customs of Much Wenlock, 1247' (*Shropshire Archaeological and Historical Society*, 66, 1989, pp. 60-2, ISSN 01435175.

19 Mumford, W. F., *Wenlock in the Middle Ages* (Shrewsbury, Mumford, 1977), ch. 6, sec. 4, 'The Priory Buildings Today', p. 89.

20 Bellamy, Vivien, *A History of Much Wenlock* (Shrewsbury, Shropshire Books, 2001), pp. 13-30.

21 Holt, R., *The Mills of Medieval England* (Oxford, Blackwell, 1988).

22 Watts, M., *Windmills* (Princes Risborough, Shire Publications, 2006), p. 1.

23 Shillingford, A. E. P., *England's Vanishing Windmills* (London, Godfrey Cave, 1979), pp. 32-3.

24 Wailes, Rex, *Windmills in England: A Study of their Origins, Development and Future* (London, Architectural Press, 1948, reprinted London, Charles Skilton, 1975), p. 11.

25 De Little, R. J., *The Windmills of England* (West Sussex, Colwood Press, 1997, 3rd ed.), p. 35.

26 Shillingford, *op. cit.*

27 NLW Wynnstay Deeds, box 43, 'Demesne Land in the Manor of Much Wenlock in County of Salop', dated 1717.

28 Rocque's Map of 1752.

29 Foxall, H. D. G., *op. cit.*

30 Seaby, W. A., and Smith, A. C., Stevenage Museum, 1984.

31 SRO Inclosure Award, B.38 & VCH, IV, The Board of Agriculture Act 1889, p. 213.

32 *History of British Landscapes and Countryside,* Part 4. www.countrylovers.co.uk/places/histland4.htm

Chapter 4

33 'GURU: Electronic Working Paper no. 35, section 4' (*University of Newcastle*).

34 Forman, W., 'Sketches of Ullesthorpe Windmill, Leics.' (1979) From Mr T. Booth collection

35 Marriott, A., 'A practising Millwright' (Cotswolds).

Chapter 5

36 Eyton, *op. cit.*, pp. 261 and 263.

37 Leighton, S., MP, FSA, *Shropshire Houses Past & Present; illustrated from drawings* (London, George Bell & Sons, 1901), p. 127.

38 Mumford, *op. cit.*, p. 84.

39 NLW Wynnstay Deeds, box E, Extracts of Grant from Queen Elizabeth to Thomas and Robert Lawley of the manor of Wenlock, 23rd Feby. Elizth.

40 NLW Wynnstay Deeds, box 43, Extracts from an indenture made thirteenth day of June in fifteenth year of the reign of Charles II, Appendix 4, Item 2), Extract 3).

41 Mumford, *op. cit.*, p. 84.

42 'A History of Shropshire: Munslow Hundred [part], The Liberty and Borough of Wenlock' from *Victoria County History*, 10, (Oxford , OUP, 1998), pp. 399-447. Also NLW Wynnstay, box 56/110 & SRO 3898/Ti if 1839 TSAS.

43 http://en.wikipedia.org/wiki/Basil_Brooke_(metallurgist)

44 Jenkins, Rhys, 'Iron-making in the Forest of Dean' (*Iron & Steel Institute*, 18 Nov. 1925).

45 Hayman, R., 'The Shropshire Wrought-iron Industry *c.*1600–1900, A Study of Technological Change' (Thesis to Centre for Lifelong Learning, The University of Birmingham, July 2003).

46 Williams, G., 'The Wenlock Limestone Industry' [A Historical Note] (Revised Edition) (1997), p. 105, p. 126.

47 NLW Wynnstay Family & Estates M2529, Extracts from a Survey of the Manor 1714.

48 Mumford, *op. cit.*, p. 73.

49 Thirsk, J. and Finberg, H. P. R., *The Agrarian History of England & Wales* (1500–1640) (Cambridge, CUP, 1967).

50 Fritze, Ronald H. and Robison, William B., eds.-in-chief, *Historical Dictionary of Stuart England (1603–1689)* (Westport, CT, Greenwood Press, 1996).

51 Freese, S., *Windmills and Millwrighting* (Cambridge, CUP, 1957, reprinted David & Charles, Newton Abbot, 1971), p. 7.

52 Morriss, R., Assessment of Buildings, Item 7.4, p. 12 of Victoria Buteux's internal article, Project 945, Report 331 'Archaeological Assessment of Much Wenlock, Shropshire' (Shropshire County Council and Hereford and Worcester County Council, May 1996, revised Dec. 1996).

53 Murchinson, Sir R. I., *The Silurian System* (London, John Murrary, 1839).

54 Clifton-Taylor, A., *The Pattern of English Building* (London, Batsford, 1962, reprinted London, Faber & Faber, 1972).

55 Hill, Richard L., *Power from Wind – A History of Windmill Technology* (Cambridge, CUP, 1st edition 1994) p. 73 and Fig. 33.

56 Fletcher, Sir Banister, *A History of Architecture* (London, Athlone Press, 1975, 18th edition), Section 32 'Renaissance Architecture in Britain 16th to 19th century'.

57 De Little, R. J., *The Windmill Yesteryear and Today* (London, John Baker, 1992), pp. 25-6 and De Little, R. J., *The Windmills of England* (West Sussex, Colwood Press, 1997, 3rd edition), p. 35.

58 Wailes, Rex, *The English Windmill* (London, Routledge and Kegan Paul, 1954), pp. 113 and 117.

59 Watts, M., *The Archaeology of Mills and Milling* (Stroud, Tempus Publishing, 2002), p. 113.

60 A. C. Norman & Co., personal publication, Sussex, May 2006.

61 Hughes, G., Broadland District Council, Sept. 2006.

62 Booth, T., Midland Wind and Watermills Group.

63 Trinder, B., *The Industrial Archaeology of Shropshire* (Chichester, Phillimore, 1996), p. 21.

Appendix 1

64 Dukes, T. F., *Antiquities of Shropshire* (Shrewsbury, 1844), p. 71.

65 An entry in 'Calendar of State Papers, Domestic Series' of reign of Charles I for 2 October, Item 13, Vol. CCLXXV – Certificate of Deputy Lieutenant of Co. Stafford, Calender of State Papers, Domestic Series, Vol. CCLXXV.

66 1636 Grant of Livery, 28 September. The National Archives/Access to Archives, Moseley Collection, Shropshire Archives 2089/1/3/7. Item 2 of contents.

67 Hull History Centre, U DDFA/26/17, Mortgage by Release: for £1600: Dame Ursula Bertye to Thomas Lawley of Twickenham esq., 2 August 1639.

68 SRO Probate Entries, 20 Nov 1671.

69 http://en.wikipedia.org/wiki/Thomas_Gage_1st_Viscount_Gage

70 NLW Wynnstay, E86 (SRO 5112/6/1).

71 McDonald, G., late Much Wenlock Town Archivist, based on material from NLW Wynnstay collection, Rental RA27, letter to W. A. Seaby & A. C. Smith at Stevenage Museum (undated).

72 East Sussex Records Office, SAS/GG/747A (1726).

73 The University of Hull (Landed Family and Estate Papers Subject Guide) http://www.hull.ac.uk/arc/collection/landed familyand estatepapers/forbes.html

74 University of Hull Brynmor Jones Library, DDfA/26/71.

75 Forester Papers.

76 Forester Papers.

77 Wenlock Olympian Society 1859 Games Programme.

78 Furbank, Muriel, Cromarty, Helen and McDonald, Glyn, *William Penny Brookes and the Olympic Connection* (Much Wenlock, Wenlock Olympian Society, 1996), back cover.

Appendix 3

79 NLW Wynnstay Deeds, box 43, no. 147, Extracts of Wenlock Estates Accounts (1647).

80 Hearne, Thomas, ed. 'The Itinerary of John Leyland' (Published from the original MS. in the Bodleian Library *c.*1710).

81 Jones, K. B., *The Wenlock Branch – Wellington to Craven Arms* (Usk, Oakwood Press, 1998), pp. 44-5.

82 Moseley Archives, 2089/1/7/21, dated 24 June 1801(Item 2 of contents).

83 NLW Wynnstay Document – Wenlock Disbursements R. A. 27, dated 1858.

84 SRO 1037 /19 1 see also Mumford, W. F. 'Terciars on the estates of Wenlock priory'. *Transactions of the Shropshire Archaeological Society*, 58.1 (1967 for 1965), 68-76.

85 The register of Sir Thomas Boteler, Much Wenlock vicar 1539–62. See also (fn 182) VCH Shropshire Vol. II Ibid. xv, p. 553. Abbot Butler did not become vicar of Much Wenlock as claimed. T.S.A.S [1st ser] vi 93; the bishop register shows that another Thomas Butler had been inducted as vicar in 1524; Reg.C. Bothe (C & YS), p. 337. See also (fn 224) VCH Shropshire Vol X. Ibid. iv (3), p. 2591; xv p. 533 Thomas Butler, elected Abbot of Shrewsbury 1529, surrendered 1540. See also S 9/808 Archives, etc. - Much Wenlock Parish Church Extracts from the Register of Sir Thomas Butler, vicar of Much Wenlock in Shropshire (Made for Private Reference in the Year 1840 by the Revd Charles Henry Hartshorne). The entry for 1553 differs slightly from the text in this document!

86 NLW Wynnstay Documents 3905/2

87 NLW Wynnstay Deeds, box E, Extracts from Copy of Grant Document of Elizabeth I.

88 NLW Wynnstay Box 43/5, 147 & Box 43/7 (1808)

89 Hull History Centre, U DDFA/26/17, Mortgage by Release: for £1600: Dame Ursula Bertye to Thomas Lawley of Twickenham esq., 2 August 1639.

90 SRO 1037/19/1 & Wynnstay 3905/2, by kind permission of the owner of The More of Linley collection (1037).

91 NLW Wynnstay Deeds, box 43, Item ii), Extracts 3) from an indenture made on thirteenth day of June in the fifteenth year of the reign of Charles II.

92 SRO Much Wenlock Probate Entry for 1709.

93 NLW Wynnstay Deeds, box 43.

94 SRO Much Wenlock Probate Entry for 1730.

95 NLW Wynnstay, MS Plans 1.

96 Royal and Sun Alliance (RSA) Insurance Group, extract from Salop Fire Office Book (with kind permission of RSA).

97 NLW Wynnstay Box 26, Deed of 1844.

98 NLW Wynnstay Document R A 27 'Wenlock Disbursements' for 1858.

Appendix 4

99 NLW Wynnsay Deeds, box E, Extracts of Grant from Queen Elizabeth to Thomas and Robert Lawley of the Manor of Wenlock, 23rd Feby 42 Elizth.

100 NLW Wynnstay Deeds, box 43, Extracts from an indenture made thirteenth day of June in the fifteenth year of the reign of Charles II.

101 NLW Wynnstay Deeds, box 43, no. 147, Extracts of Estate Accounts of Wenlock in 1647.

102 NLW Wynnstay Deeds, box 43, no. 82, Extracts from the full transcript of Will and Testament of Robert Bertie and Mr Gage's Title, 1699.

103 NLW Wynnstay Family and Estates, M2529, Extracts from a Survey of the Manor, 1714.

104 http://www.1911encyclopedia.org/Copyhold

Acknowledgements

Funding assistance for the initial stage of tower preservation was gratefully received from Bridgnorth District Council, Shropshire Hills Area of Outstanding Natural Beauty (SHAONB) Partnership and the Midland Wind and Watermills Group.

The Trust also received a Parish Pump Priming Award.

A number of local organisations, including D & M Evans Steel Fabrications, RBS Construction, Cambers Agricultural Suppliers and Wenlock Fencing, generously provided labour and/or materials for use on the project.

Mr C Ship, an ex-chairman of the Trust, kindly provided the scaffolding steelwork.

The Trust also recognises the assistance provided by Mr D Norrey for constructing and installing the new doors and window shutters and to C & S Gregory for repointing the external stonework.

The Trust is extremely grateful for all these contributions.

On behalf of Much Wenlock Windmill Trust, the author wishes to record the Trust's appreciation to Mr Peter Lewis (Asterley Mill) for his advice in the early stages of my pursuit of this project and to Mr Gareth Hughes (Broadland District Council and the Society for the Protection of Ancient Buildings (SPAB), Wind and Watermills Section) for his thorough review of and comments on the physical data provided by the author.

The contribution of Mr Tim Booth (Midland Wind and Watermills Group) and Jean Lawley at New Hall Mill (Sutton Coldfield) greatly assisted in directing the search for historical material.

Grateful thanks go to Mr Adam Marriott (Cotswold millwright) for his advice and comments on previously presented assumptions from the author; these comments have been noted and the text updated accordingly.

Thanks are also due to Will Motley for confirming the family details included in the text and also to Lady Forester for the kind permission to view selected estate documents. The advice and assistance of Helen Haynes (senior archivist) and staff at Shropshire Archives have been invaluable.

The material extracted from the Wynnstay manuscripts is by permission of Llyfrgell Genedlaethol Cymru/The National Library of Wales. The archives departments at the University of Hull Brynmor Jones Library and Lincolnshire Archives, and Mrs Heather Hedges, Much Wenlock librarian, have all made significant contributions and been extremely helpful in the provision of relevant material.

The advice and support material regarding design and conservation issues supplied by Mr Philip MacDowell, area surveyor, West Sussex County Council, is much appreciated.

The excellent photography included in the book provided by Sabine Hutchinson (Virtual Shropshire) and Mr J Moore has been of immense value.

My personal thanks go to the Trustees who assisted in the provision of printing consumables throughout the preparation of this book.

Mr Dave Lloyd's knowledge, experience and practical skill in the building trade have been invaluable in successful completion of the initial stages of tower preservation.

Sincere thanks go to my publishers, the editor and the graphics designer for their contributions in making this book presentable, and to Mr H Goldsack for his expertise in the presentation of the very important inscription dates.

The author has referred to numerous providers of primary and secondary source material in the preparation of this book and every attempt has been made to appropriately acknowledge all of the material accessed.

Every effort has been made to contact the copyright holders of material. If any copyrights have been overlooked, the author will be pleased to make the necessary arrangements.

Picture credits

The author is grateful to the following for the use of their images:

Sue Adair p. 52
Sabine Hutchinson pp. cover, p. 3, p. 31 lower, p. 32
Mr J Moore p. 63
Victoria County History, map reproduced from *A History of Shropshire* Vol. X. (Oxford University Press, 1998), p. 411, by permission of the Director p. 82
Wenlock Olympian Society p. 65
www.flickr.com/photos/idodds/119431894/2006 pp. 26

All other photographs are the author's.

From the Album